MY SCOTLAND

BY ITS FAMOUS SONS AND DAUGHTERS

EDITED BY
ANNE GRAHAM AND MICHAEL HAMILTON

DESIGN BY JEREMY HOPES

KingfisherReach
Publishing Ltd

Published by Kingfisher Reach Publishing Ltd
Northumberland
my-scotland.org

First published in 2015

978-0-9576897-1-8

Printed and bound in Scotland by Bell & Bain Ltd

Distributed by BookSource

CONTENTS

Ronni Ancona 4-7

Gary Anderson 8-11

Ian Anderson 12-15

Aly Bain 16-19

Nicola Benedetti 20-23

Rory Bremner 24-27

Craig Brown 28-31

Jack Bruce 32-35

Gordon Buchanan 36-39

Eilidh Child 40-43

Pat Clinton 44-47

Brian Cox 48-51

Christine De Luca 52-55

Barbara Dickson 56-59

Donovan 60-63

Karen Dunbar 64-67

Fish 68-71

Laura Fraser 72-75

Katherine Grainger 76-79

John Greig 80-83

Clare Grogan 84-87

Cat Harvey 88-91

Armando Iannucci 92-95

Jim Kerr 96-99

Ross King 100-103

Declan Michael Laird 104-107

Denis Law 108-111

Sue Lawrence 112-115

Denis Lawson 116-119

Phyllis Logan 120-123

Sir Malcolm MacGregor 124-127

Donald John Mackay 128-131

Hugh MacLeod 132-135

Val McDermid 136-139

Jim McLean 140-143

Billy McNeill 144-147

Peter Morrison 148-151

David Moyes 152-155

Eve Muirhead 156-159

Judy Murray 160-163

Nick Nairn 164-167

Daniela Nardini 168-171

Rab Noakes 172-175

Oor Wullie 176-179

Bill Paterson 180-183

Gail Porter 184-187

Eddi Reader 188-191

Jean Redpath 192-195

James Robertson 196-199

Andy Scott 200-203

Dougray Scott 204-207

John Gordon Sinclair 208-211

Sir Jackie Stewart 212-215

Janette Tough 216-219

Midge Ure 220-223

Jack Vettriano 224-227

Sheena Wellington 228-231

Irvine Welsh 232-235

RONNI ANCONA

actress, impressionist, author

Ronni came to prominence in the top-rating BBC show The Big Impression *with Alistair McGowan – for which she won Best TV Comedy Actress Award in 2003 – and has acted in many straight roles, recently in* Last Tango in Halifax. *Ronni is also an author, with* A Matter of Life and Death: How to Wean a Man off Football *to her name.*

I WAS PASSIONATE ABOUT BEING SCOTS when I was a child. I was in a Gaelic choir – although I was probably the worst singer in it – and I loved Scottish country dancing. Hogmanay was the best time of the year, with excited kids running around from house to house. There was always a fantastic atmosphere, and I've never found the magic of that again. These days, for me, what really defines Scottishness is the people's dark sense of humour and dry wit. And it's a humour that travels well: just look at all the successful comics that have come out of Scotland.

As my father was in the Navy, we were always moving around when I was growing up in Scotland, so I got to experience different ways of life in different areas. My first years were in Lossiemouth but I don't remember much about that time, except that my mother used to buy my vests in Inverness!

I was still little when we moved to Cramond near the Firth of Forth and I have a lot of good memories from that time. My mum and I used to walk round the Roman ruins and I would pretend I was baking cakes on the big stone slabs. I went to the local primary school where I could let my imagination run riot. One day the class was painting flowers and I painted a big demon flower with teeth in black and burgundy colours. I got covered in paint and pretended I was a monster. I had this mop of candyfloss hair and the teacher used to call me her little Shetland pony. She kept kirby grips just for me.

We moved to Troon in Ayrshire when I was six and that was a big shock: everything at school was much more strict and my writing paper with dogs and cats on it was frowned upon. My father was into old cars and he

"I loved walking on the beach at Troon with our two cocker spaniels."

insisted on taking us around in his 1950s wooden station wagon: I was perpetually mortified. In Troon everything was about golf and we were never really into it. My father used to shout at the Tannoy on the municipal course and tell it to shut up. But there was always a great excitement when the Open came to town and everyone got caught up in it.

As a youngster you often live in your imagination. On a clear day in Troon I'd look across the sea to the Isle of Arran and, occasionally, you could just about glimpse the lower tip of Ireland. I used to imagine it was New York.

I loved walking on the beach with our two cocker spaniels, Candy and Muffin. My friends and I would collect bottles of Irn Bru and cream soda from the beach and return them for money so we could buy our own bottle. We were never allowed loads of sweets – my mother used to divide up Jelly Tots, and ice cream was something you'd only have as a special treat in the summer when you were on holiday. And everyone wanted

"On a clear day in Troon I'd look across the sea to the Isle of Arran and, occasionally, you could just about glimpse the lower tip of Ireland."
Sunset over the Isle of Arran from the Ballast Bank, Troon

tablet – a kind of Scottish fudge – which was the biggest treat of all.

Life seemed pretty simple back then. We never went abroad for holidays: everyone would go to the Highlands or the coast or a loch – but wherever you went it was always beautiful. Not that kids care that much about beautiful scenery. Loch Trool is a lovely spot in Galloway but my clearest memory from our caravan holiday there was the midges. We had a tent outside and they were just everywhere – you couldn't escape them. My dad used to carry us around in our sleeping bags so we didn't get bitten and we would burn joss sticks to keep the midges at bay – not that my parents were hippies, sadly. Another time Dad took us to the John O'Groats Hotel in the wooden station wagon, and now the hotel has a photo of it on the front of their menu.

The most exhilarating experience for me in those days was going to Glasgow in the winter when the pantomimes were on, battling through the snow and – the height of sophistication – eating a Danish pastry in the House of Fraser on the way.

My mother used to do the scenery at Glasgow Theatre Royal and I can remember as if it was yesterday the workshop, the stink of glue and the old paints cooking on Calor Gas. I loved that world. I was a shy child, but a bit of a show-off when it came to performance (I remember when myself and two friends called ourselves Pot's People and we'd perform on a TV set made out of cardboard) so I felt at home in that environment of the theatre. Everyone used to go to the panto then, whatever their background. I used to worship Stanley Baxter, and I loved Rikki Fulton and Jack Milroy. I was obsessed with Scottish 'camp'. It upsets me when people are rude about Glasgow. I love it and, for me as a child, it represented the highest form of exoticism.

Glasgow Theatre Royal before redevelopment

GARY ANDERSON

darts player

Dubbed 'The Flying Scotsman', Gary was crowned world champion in the 2015 Professional Darts Corporation (PDC) annual championship in London's Alexandra Palace, beating English darts legend Phil Taylor. He went on to win the PDC Player of the Year award in the same year. He has won several major titles and has been world number one for both the British Darts Organisation and the World Darts Federation.

I NEVER EVEN PICKED UP A DART until I was 24, and it was purely by chance. I used to enjoy playing snooker and pool but it cost you 50p or £1 a time. I hadn't much money in my pocket and having a game of darts was free, so I gave it a go. I just found it easy, really enjoyed it and carried on from there. The only thing I found hard was doing all the calculations to work out which double to go for. I remember in those very early days one of the boys telling me that one day I'd be world champion, but I never gave it any thought at the time. I certainly never thought I'd make any kind of living from it.

So I carried on my job making fire grates for the Fireplace Studio in Portobello, Edinburgh where I worked for 19 years. I was quite happy working during the day and playing darts afterwards.

I'd play in pubs and clubs, making 20 quid here, £50 there and I joined the county league and Superleague in Falkirk. I managed to get straight into the six-man Scotland team in my first year in the counties. I was so proud to be picked to play for my country.

I never had a coach or anything. Maybe some of the other pros do, but I keep myself to myself. I'm my own coach. It's not that difficult to me – it's just throwing three pointy things at a board! I've been trying to get one of my sons to play and I keep asking him: "Why are you going across there?" when he goes to the wrong place on the board. I suppose what's natural to me isn't natural to other people.

The thing you have to work on is the pressure, but the longer you play the more you get used to it. If you're playing well and you've got the crowd behind you nothing upsets you. But when you're struggling you hear

Gary and his manager Tommy Gilmour celebrate his world championship win in 2015

"Although I live in Somerset now I go back to Scotland as much as I can – to Musselburgh where I was born and brought up."

Gary in action

every voice at the back. It's just a question of getting back to your job and not letting your concentration lapse.

Sometimes as a Scotsman playing in places like London you can get a bit of a niggle from the crowd, but the audience were fantastic when I won the world title, even though I was playing Phil Taylor who is the game's finest. You will never see the like of him again. When he is absolutely determined to win, trust me, he will win.

We get on very well together and have done for years, but when you get up on stage you're on your own, and you have no friends. In the final I had some bad luck, like when three darts fell out of treble 20. I thought that was it, that it wasn't my day, but when we got to 6-6 something kicked in and I realised I could do it.

When you're on stage you forget that what you are doing is affecting the people behind you. It's probably more nerve-racking for my partner Rachel than for me. My manager Tommy Gilmour isn't even allowed to watch darts in his house because he gets so nervous, but he was at Alexandra Palace for the tournament. I think he took a week's blood pressure tablets in one night. He's based in Glasgow and keeps my feet on the ground.

Being world champion is a great thing, but if it hadn't been for all the attention and interviews afterwards I'd have just moved on to the next tournament. That's how darts is.

Maybe it's something to do with the Scottish character: you enjoy the moment then you get on with the rest of your life.

You also remember the bad times and you see how easily it could not have happened. A few years ago I lost my father and one of my brothers very close to each other and it was devastating for me. It felt like I lost two years. But everyone was great and understanding and I got off my backside and went back to work. When I won the title, I like to think my dad and brother were having a pint together to celebrate!

Although I live in Somerset now I go back to Scotland as much as I can – to Musselburgh where I was born and brought up and to Tranent to see my mum and other family. I'm a true Scot, and I bleed blue and white. The best sight for me is when I'm driving home and I see the Scotland sign on the Borders.

And if there's one piece of music that means 'home' to me it's *Flower of Scotland*. It makes every hair on your body stand on end, even if you've heard it a million times.

"The best sight sight for me is when I'm driving home and I see the Scotland sign on the Borders."
A piper at Carter Bar

IAN ANDERSON MBE
musician

Best known as the charismatic flautist and singer in Jethro Tull, Ian has worked as a recording and performing musician since the 1960s. Jethro Tull, formed in 1968, released 30 studio and live albums, selling more than 60 million copies since the band first performed at London's famous Marquee Club. Ian also has a solo career and released his album Homo Erraticus *in 2014.*

I WAS BORN IN DUNFERMLINE to a mother from Manchester and a father from Fife, and I consider myself an archetypal Brit, genetically speaking. I celebrate both my Scottish and my English origins. I am the epitome of the guy who enjoys the union of Scotland and England. For me it would have been sad if, after 300 years of union and a huge symbiotic relationship, it had come to an end.

I recorded *A Wee Deoch an Doris* – a farewell drink before you say good night – for an album of Scottish songs because that's how I felt about the possible end of the union. It would have been a sad goodbye for me.

Obviously I grew up feeling quite Scottish, although not as Scottish as other kids in the school. The boys played football and liked rough sports. I didn't really fit in with that, being more of an artsy pre-pubescent. I used to sit at the back of the class with the girls because we were the ones who were academic 'try harders'. I got on better with the girls. Ironically I was quite good at football but I declined to take part in any team either in primary or grammar school.

I think sport is great when it's fun but I wasn't one for winning at any cost or doing anything that involved cheating.

I went to Roseburn Primary School in Edinburgh and I was all set to go to Edinburgh Royal High – I even had all my uniform – when my parents decided to up sticks and move to Blackpool where they had met. I don't know what happened to that uniform – I never got to wear it. Maybe it's on eBay. It was a big wrench for me.

When we got there suddenly I stood out. People would call me Jock. I didn't want to fake anything but

Ian pictured in 2014 with his band

I did my best to lose the accent; I was aiming for something quite neutral.

My best memories of Scotland are of the west coast sailing paddle steamers down the Clyde, trips round the borders, the Firth of Forth and especially Edinburgh. When I think of Scotland that's the place that always comes first to mind. When I go back I travel the number 41 bus to Cramond where I used to go a lot with my brother who had boats and loved to sail.

I had a business in Skye and have a strong connection with it though, for me, it was a work environment. But Edinburgh is somewhere I could live; it has great culture and industry and really feels like a capital city. It has an aura about it. My brothers chose to make their home in Glasgow, but Edinburgh is still the place I proudly talk about anywhere in the world. If people say they'd like to visit the UK I tell them to make sure to visit Scotland, of course, but especially Edinburgh.

My musical influences weren't Scottish at all but urban black American musicians like Muddy Waters and Howlin' Wolf. But later in life when I was about 20 I started to appreciate folk, classical, big band jazz and church music – I began following my more European nose.

It's definitely the case that, for many Scots, a lot of us have to leave Scotland to realise what it means to us. We have to step away to see its true worth. I suppose I'm part of the great Scottish diaspora. Andrew Carnegie was recognised more as Scots in his life and work abroad. I have played at Carnegie Hall in New York and there is one in Dunfermline which I used to suppose pre-dated the one in New York. But it doesn't – it's new. And I'm pleased to say I've played both.

As far as Scottish characteristics go, I think we have a lot in common with north-western culture – with people like Norwegians and Icelanders. I'm probably something of a product of Celtic wool-weavers and Vikings.

There's a huge number of Polish, Estonian, Ukrainian and other nationalities who have come to live and work in Scotland. They have brought their own culture to Scotland and I think we're the better for it.

Looking back at the old Scottish culture I can appreciate with a smile on my face the poetry of Robbie Burns. I even have affection for William McGonagall; he was the world's worst poet but his work still survives. He's the Eddie the Eagle of poetry – and I think it's good that we can celebrate spectacular failures.

jethrotull.com

"Edinburgh is the place I proudly talk about."
Scott Monument

"I have played at Carnegie Hall in New York, and there is one in Dunfermline which I used to suppose pre-dated the one in New York. But it doesn't – it's new. And I'm pleased to say I've played both."
Carnegie Hall, Dunfermline

15

ALY BAIN MBE
fiddle player

Aly Bain is one of the finest fiddle players Scotland has ever produced. Early in his career he formed The Humblebums with Billy Connolly and Gerry Rafferty, then The Boys of the Lough whom he played with for 30 years. In 1994 he was awarded the MBE for services to music. In 2013 the BBC Radio 2 Folk Awards honoured his lifetime achievement. He still tours with accordion player and composer Phil Cunningham.

I WAS BORN IN LERWICK, SHETLAND nine months after World War Two finished – luckily for me. Lerwick at that time was a busy herring port, probably the biggest in Europe. My father was a cooper and during the winter made barrels ready to fill with salt herring. He made up to nine barrels every day and was a truly great craftsman. He worked alone all winter in his little cooperage. It was a hard trade. He would work stripped to the waist and had a physique any bodybuilder would be proud of.

As a boy I remember the smells of wood shavings and the fires he lit to steam the barrel staves over. During the summer – when the herring was landed – fish gutters and coopers came from all over Scotland and parts of Ireland. They all lived in huts belonging to the various curing stations of which there were many. My father would tie me on to the end of the pier as I loved to fish. I knew all the gutters and coopers and for the first time got to know dialects from other parts of the country.

If I wasn't with Dad I would be in Sandwick, in the south of Shetland, fishing for trout in the burns and lochs. Shetland was my life and my childhood was like a dream. I was only in the house to eat and sleep. The rest was a huge adventure. Holidays involved going to the country staying with my aunts and uncles. I didn't leave the island until I was 14 when I went to school camp in Midlothian. Then for the first time I saw forests, rivers, trains and cities. It was a lot to take in – all in just ten days.

My interest in music started at an early age. My parents lived in a flat next to Tom Anderson, who was a great fiddler. I heard him play all the time and it must have stayed with me. When I was 11 my parents got me a fiddle and I went to Tom for lessons. The island at that time was full of players. It seemed like almost everyone could make some kind of tune on the instrument. I learned quickly and was soon playing at school concerts and local dances.

In the days before TV, Shetland was a completely different place. People just wandered in and out of each other's houses. If you could play the fiddle you were in demand and welcomed into most houses any time. The main forms of entertainment were playing music or playing cards. There were stories aplenty as men had travelled all over the world in the Navy. Growing up in Shetland taught me all about people. Shetland is like a miniature world made up of all kinds of people. We had time to get to know each other, and look out for each other.

The beach at Durness

"I love the islands of course, and being near the sea. My favourite part of the mainland is the north west. The drive between Ullapool and Durness is wild and beautiful."

17

Aly with Phil Cunningham

When I lived in Shetland I was a Shetlander. Scotland was far away and we felt independent of the mainland. In those days our life was the sea. Boats came and went. The sea was our gateway to the world. When I moved to the mainland in 1968 it was a very different world from the one in which I grew up.

I moved to Glasgow to stay with my brother and his family. To be in the heart of industrial Scotland was quite a change from the peace and quiet and clean air of Shetland. Being a time-served joiner I was a member of the working class but in Glasgow that took on a whole different meaning. Radical was the word, and I loved it.

My first agent was Arthur Argo who convinced me to try and make a living from music. He worked as a producer for Radio Scotland and his main interest was traditional music. He came from a famous family of north-east Scotland music collectors. Arthur already had a few artists on his books – including Billy Connolly and Barbara Dickson – who were both, like me, just starting out. Although I found it strange being on the mainland, I quickly got to love it. We were at the beginning of a revival of our culture the likes of which had never been seen before.

I feel my music is a treasure handed down and evolved over centuries. When I play I feel where I belong. It's in my bones. I could never leave this country in life or death. Why would I?

I'm very proud to be Scots. I've travelled the world over and know I live in one of the most beautiful countries on earth. I also love the people, who are honest and down-to-earth. I love the islands of course, and being near the sea. My favourite part of the mainland is the north-west. The drive between Ullapool and Durness is wild and beautiful. Around every corner it's like a picture postcard.

My home has been Edinburgh for over 40 years now. I love waking up at home and walking round the city, I think it's one of the most beautiful cities in the world. I never tire of seeing the architecture and stonework. For me it's full of memories of the great friends I have, and have had. Two of my daughters live in Edinburgh and my two grandsons. It's home indeed.

The 'No' vote, I have to say, shook me to the core. It's something I'll never understand although I'll keep trying. I come from a radical left-wing family where politics was discussed every day. My brother at one time worked full-time for the Communist party. My parents were socialists. I joined the SNP as I felt the Labour Party left me a while ago. The great Jimmy Reid – who I knew and loved – inspired me with his fertile mind and love of working people. To my mind he was a great Scotsman. Now, as I get older and look back at my life, I wouldn't change a thing. Except Margaret Thatcher.

philandaly.com

"My home has been Edinburgh for over 40 years now. I love waking up at home and walking round the city, I think it's one of the most beautiful cities in the world. I never tire of seeing the architecture and stonework."

19

NICOLA BENEDETTI MBE
classical violinist

Since starting out with the National Youth Orchestra of Scotland, Nicola has become one of the world's best-known violinists. She won the UK's Brilliant Prodigy competition in 2002 and was the BBC's Young Musician of the Year in 2004. She has played with the Royal Scottish National Orchestra and the Royal Philharmonic and she appeared in the 2012 Last Night of the Proms. Nicola has also released many albums including Homecoming – A Scottish Fantasy.

I WAS A SEASIDE CHILD. I was brought up in West Kilbride – where my family still live – so my whole childhood was spent by the sea. I grew up with beautiful views and lots of space in a place with a very village type of feeling. My family is Italian/Scottish and we were all very close. We spent a lot of time together.

Looking back, my most vivid memories are of the house where my mother grew up on the outskirts of the Auchinleck Estate near Mauchline. My Italian grandmother and Scottish grandfather had this tiny cottage on the edge of the estate. There were beautiful, enormous stately homes within the estate but also hundreds of acres open to everyone. The grounds were wild and wonderful with a lot of mini-glens, unbelievable vegetation and general beauty. It was like a dream world in the countryside.

We would go there after school and also at weekends. We would go for long walks, maybe for five to six hours, with my mother's brothers who lived there. We'd be out in the thick of the Scottish countryside and we used to take all the neighbours' dogs with us. Within the estate there were a couple of ancient caves which were said to have been used by William Wallace. My uncle would always give us a history lesson on every walk. It got us integrated into the fabric of Scotland.

It was a very unfancy, grounding upbringing and my experience of Scotland then was very much of the outdoors. Scottish people are very proud of that aspect of the country. People grow up making an effort to go out and enjoy the land around them.

Of course we had the Italian part of our lives too, and our holidays were usually in Italy or sometimes France. But Scotland is where I'm from. I love it and am proud of it but I'm not one who thinks that, because I'm Scottish, Scotland is somehow a higher country than any other. But it does have its unique qualities that come from the very distinctive nature of the people. I know many first-time visitors to Scotland think it is going to feel just like England – but it doesn't. They're not necessarily prepared for the dramatically different nature of Scottish personalities. Scots are extremely straightforward – sometimes to the point of dryness – but I've been told by many people that after a while they are very relaxed in Scotland.

> **❝ I am always more relaxed in Scotland than anywhere else**

There are very few layers to get through to get to what they are fundamentally. I certainly find that and I am always more relaxed in Scotland than anywhere else. Take the fame thing. I have a job that is very public so obviously people do recognise me, but when I go to airports in Scotland, for example, all anyone says to me is: "How's it going, Nicky?" No one makes a fuss. I remember in America once a young girl burst into tears when she met me. That would never happen to me in Scotland! Here the attitude is "you're just one of us" and that absolutely gives you a very healthy perspective and keeps you grounded.

Politically, historically and philosophically there is embedded in Scotland a real belief in equality. You find

Nicola reopened Portencross Castle in West Kilbride in 2010

that sentiment in abundance there. It's something I have carried with me into what has become, for me, a very international life. When you look at the world and all its complexity that belief is something I will always take with me. It's something you notice even more when you move away because you don't find it everywhere.

Scotland will always be home, but I live close to Heathrow Airport in London because it's so practical. I spend so much time travelling that it's a necessity, really. But I still spend such a huge amount of time in Scotland doing concerts and seeing family that I don't really feel I have ever moved away.

The place that I always have in mind when I'm away is the view from my parents' house across the sea to Arran. I probably have hundreds of photos in my phone

of the changing views and beautiful sunsets. It's just stunning. Another place that has very special memories for me is Usher Hall in Edinburgh. It was there that I won the BBC Young Musician of the Year award when I was 16, and I think that it was only the second time I had performed there. I have very positive associations with that place.

Obviously classical music is what I do, what drives me and what I strive to constantly do better. Awards are lovely to get, but my proudest moments are when I go on stage and I do something better than I have done it before. You will never find a happier Nicky than at those moments. And the great thing about music is that you can get better as you get older. It's not a linear journey; it's extremely varied and when you feel you've reached a

new high point it's wonderful.

I really enjoy playing with folk musicians like Aly Bain, Phil Cunningham and Julie Fowlis. They are masters in their field. When you're studying violin and classical music you are encouraged to avoid mixing styles like classical and folk which is a shame. Our education categorises and separates traditions that were never that far apart. The story of the music, whatever it is, is a marvellous thing, and as musicians we can play our part in humanising these stories for our audience.

nicolabenedetti.co.uk

@NickyBenedetti

"Usher Hall in Edinburgh has very special memories for me. It was there that I won the BBC Young Musician of the Year award when I was 16."

RORY BREMNER
satirist and impressionist

After working on the London cabaret comedy circuit, Rory moved into television. He has featured in shows from Spitting Image *and* Mock the Week *to* Bremner, Bird and Fortune. *For two decades he hosted his own award-winning C4 series* Rory Bremner…Who Else? *Rory was a* Strictly Come Dancing *contestant in 2011 and has translated operas including* Carmen *and* The Silver Lake. *His contribution to the Scottish Referendum debate was* Rory Goes to Holyrood, *a satirical look at Scottish politics.*

I HAD PAVEMENT UNDER MY FEET for most of my childhood, having been born and brought up in Edinburgh. It was a sheltered, middle-class upbringing, something I only fully realised years later. It was as genteel as you might expect, living in Morningside – with ladies nearby who were so posh they make the Queen look like she lives on *Benefits Street* (which I suppose she does, in a way).

We lived near Holy Corner – so called because there are three churches there, including Christ Church, where I was a choirboy. I went to Gillsland Park prep school, then to Clifton Hall in Newbridge, a boarding school where I was happy but used to imagine running back home. That wasn't an option at my next school – Wellington College in Berkshire.

Edinburgh is my home town, and every time I go back it moves me. I just love it. As a teenager, I used to work in the George Hotel as a night porter. I would walk home at five in the morning and breathe in the city around me. I'd walk from George Street over Princes Street, up The Mound, past Greyfriars Bobby and across the Meadows. I also love Blackford Hill where you can see the whole sweep of the city below – from the Forth bridges to the west, over Edinburgh's Old Town, the Castle, Salisbury Crags, Arthur's Seat, right round towards Musselburgh and the east coast. It's a fabulous view.

I love Edinburgh's duality, set in stone in the tall tenements of the Old Town and the Georgian pomp of the New Town, designed by the 26-year-old James Craig and home to the city's lawyers and financiers. Then there's the darker, seamier, seedier side – the Leith of Irvine

Welsh's *Trainspotting*. Robert Louis Stevenson made the two personalities flesh in *Dr Jekyll and Mr Hyde*. And while the celebrated anatomist Robert Knox lectured in the city in the 1820s, his specimens were provided by the low-life murderers Burke and Hare.

I studied French and German at King's College London at a time when London's alternative cabaret scene was really taking off in the 1980s. That's where my political education really started. I had my eyes opened and a lot of middle-class naivety knocked out of me by some very bright, political comedians like Tony Allen, Mark Steel, Alexei Sayle and Jeremy Hardy. Many of Britain's top comedians emerged from the Edinburgh Fringe Festivals of the late 1970s and early 1980s – Rowan Atkinson, Stephen Fry, Hugh Laurie, Emma Thompson, Tony Slattery, Griff Rhys Jones, Angus Deayton, Clive Anderson, even a young Rik Mayall.

My passport to the world of satire was my love of impressions, which goes right back to childhood in Edinburgh, watching Stanley Baxter in panto at the King's Theatre and marvelling at the talent and spectacle of his shows (and his legs!).

I always loved coming back to Edinburgh to do the festival. The posters for my first big show featured me naked except for a pair of glasses – the idea being that you didn't need props. God knows what my mother and her friends thought of it. I wasn't comfortable going back to perform at the festival once I was an established act. I felt it was for new performers trying to get a break and I didn't want to queer the pitch for them. Maybe I was being over-sensitive. But festival or no festival, I always

"Edinburgh is my home town, and every time I go back it moves me. I just love it."

"Spean Bridge, a few miles north of Fort William, where the commando monument overlooks the roads with Ben Nevis in the background, is the most fabulously beautiful landscape."

"The view around Smailholm Tower near Kelso, with the Eildon hills in the background, is sensational."

As a result, I spend a large part of my time in fields watching ponies. The Border folk are genuine and friendly, with a great sense of perspective and humour. During the Referendum campaign, I was at a country show in Duns where there was a 'Yes' tent and a 'No' tent. I eavesdropped outside each one. The people in the 'Yes' tent were talking about the future. In the 'No' tent they were fussing about currency. I spotted a Lib Dem tent, and went to listen. As I approached the tent, I heard a voice inside saying: "So how are your tomatoes, Donald?" You couldn't make stuff like that up.

Tessa's family live near Hawick, and we married there. Border folk are very proud of their landscape and their history. The minister who married us took me to a hilltop above the town. I said it was like being shown the promised land, but with cashmere and tweed instead of milk and honey. Before I moved here, I used to think that scenery began at Perth. I don't any more: the low hills and big skies of the Borders are just as beautiful. The view around Smailholm Tower near Kelso, with the Eildon hills in the background, is sensational.

Sometimes I escape for a game of golf, either in the Borders or at St Andrews, a favourite childhood haunt (eggs and bacon in a B&B overlooking the sea.) The caddies are real characters, especially, if, like me, you manage to hit the ball into the middle of a huge gorse bush. ("Ye could wrap that up in bacon, sir, and Lassie'd no find it!")

Wherever I am, I've always felt emotionally Scottish – and never more so than against the English at rugby. We all know that 1990, when Scotland won at Murrayfield, was the only game that mattered. It was the time of Thatcher's poll tax – trialled in Scotland – and feelings were raw. It felt as if Will Carling and his team were representing Tory England. And, as the song says, "We sent 'em homeward, tae think again."

@rorybremner

enjoy being back in the city. There is something about retracing your footsteps from your youth, reliving your memories from the perspective of a much older person. Going back to a kind of innocence after everything you've experienced since.

I moved back to Scotland a few years ago when my children were eight and six. I was filming a BBC documentary about Scottish soldiers. As ever (control freak!), I insisted on driving the BBC Land Rover. We filmed at Spean Bridge, a few miles north of Fort William, where the commando monument overlooks the roads with Ben Nevis in the background – the most fabulously beautiful landscape. Then we drove on to just a few miles shy of Oban and stopped at an oyster bar. It was baking hot (Billy Connolly used to say Scotland has two seasons – winter and July – but this was June!) and we stopped to enjoy oysters, fresh langoustines and Guinness. That was just for starters. Then we went on into Oban and found

a place by the harbour. When we came out at about quarter to 11 it was still light. As a blue twilight fell, a school of dolphins came out to play in the bay beyond the harbour. That's when I knew I wanted my children to understand that this was their country, their heritage. It's beautiful and it's where they come from. And, for me, it felt like the right time to fully renew my ties.

My wife Tessa grew up in the Borders. We bought a lovely old mansion house there and have spent ages doing it up. It's near Kelso and Jedburgh. Horse country. Reiver country. With two young daughters, life's all about ponies – childhood is so short, and we wanted the girls to have the kind of childhood that Tessa had, where the biggest event of the day was jumping across a stream – or into one – and eating sausage rolls in the back of a horsebox. We also wanted to let them enjoy freedom in the countryside.

"I used to think that scenery began at Perth. I don't any more: the low hills and big skies of the Borders are just as beautiful." The Eildon hills seen from Scott's View, Scottish Borders

CRAIG BROWN CBE
football manager

Craig managed the Scottish football team from 1993-2001 and he holds the distinction of having the longest tenure for a Scottish manager, presiding over 70 games. Under him Scotland qualified for Euro '96 and the 1998 World Cup in France. After a playing career cut short by injury, he also managed Aberdeen, Motherwell, Preston North End and Clyde. In 1999 he was awarded a CBE for services to football.

I'M OLD ENOUGH TO HAVE VIVID MEMORIES of the Second World War because I was born in 1940. My earliest memory is being carried out to the air-raid shelter. I can hear the siren to this day. If we couldn't get out to the shelter in time my mother would put me under the table and lie on top of me.

All the people would be singing *Onward Christian Soldiers*. It was far from ideal but there was a great community spirit. Half a banana was a weekly treat. The tenement houses in Corkerhill – which was the railway village in Glasgow – didn't have bathrooms. You went to the community centre for a bath twice a week. I can still smell the carbolic soap.

My dad was away in the RAF for five years serving as a parachute instructor. When he came back in 1945 here was this man you didn't know coming into the house in uniform. To a five-year-old that was terrifying. We moved to Hamilton when I was about seven or eight. I have fond memories of Hamilton Academy. It was one of the best schools in the country academically. Football and golf were always my sports at school and I wanted to be a PE teacher when I left.

We always took our holidays in Scotland. You didn't go to Majorca for your holidays in the 1950s. The beautiful isle of Arran was a favourite, about an hour's sailing from Ardrossan. One of my favourite views is looking across the bay over the Holy Isle towards the Ayrshire coast from Lamlash golf course. I have two brothers, and for teenage boys it was golf every day and diving off the pier into the freezing waters. Idyllic.

Although I live in Aberdeen now – I'm a director of the club – I did live in Prestwick and Ayr for a while and I

"One of my favourite views is looking across the bay over the Holy Isle towards the Ayrshire coast from Lamlash golf course."

"I have two brothers, and for teenage boys it was golf every day and diving off Lamlash pier into the freezing waters. Idyllic."

have two sons and a daughter who still live there. I really love the Ayrshire coast and the links golf courses: Turnberry, Royal Troon and Prestwick where the first Open was played. I particularly love the views at Turnberry. My son is a member at Royal Troon so I sometimes get a game there although I'm a member of St. Nicholas Golf Club in Prestwick, which is a superb links course.

I played football for the Scottish schoolboys and was lucky enough to be friendly with two of the greats of Scottish football – Billy McNeill and Alex Ferguson – and we have stayed friends through the years. I was a good schoolboy player but joining Rangers in 1958 was a bit of a mistake because I wasn't really good enough to get into the first team. Jim Baxter was a good friend from those days at Ibrox, but I was a bit neglected and when you got an injury the treatment wasn't really adequate then.

I was never going to make enough money as a footballer so the PE teaching fitted in nicely with the playing, and later when I was a manager. My knee injuries cut short my playing days. I had five operations in a few years and in those days a cartilage op meant a week in hospital. These days it's keyhole surgery and you are up and about the same day.

An education official at Dundee upset me but did me a real favour when he took me aside and told me PE teachers were regarded as ignorant acrobats! That gave me the impetus to get some academic respectability. The Open University had just started so I took an Arts degree. I had a busy schedule studying, teaching and playing for Falkirk in the mid-1960s, but by the time I finished playing in 1967 I was multi-qualified. I left teaching in 1986 after 22 years and 76 days to join the SFA as U21 coach and assistant national coach to Andy Roxburgh.

I took over the Scottish team in 1993. My proudest moment is managing the Scottish team, playing the opening game of the World Cup in France against the world champions Brazil, with 111 countries and however many billions watching us live on TV. At the time you don't realise the magnitude of it because you are just doing your job. It's only as the years go by and you reflect on things when you realise that was quite special.

Although I'm a great fan of Scottish country music I also love Rod Stewart and his songs like *Sailing*. When we were going to the Mexico World Cup we had a warm-up game in Los Angeles where he lives and he invited the whole team to his house. It was only four days before the opening game and Alex Ferguson who was the manager was worried about how such a visit would affect the lads and refused to let them go. Rod's parties are legendary.

I don't know any Scot who isn't proud to be Scottish. There's a Scottish word – couthiness – that sums up the Scottish character perfectly. There's an agreeable, kindly quality about the Scots. The support you get at a family and community level is a microcosm of the support the national team players get representing their country. I've travelled the world and people everywhere admire the Scots because of their camaraderie. It's exemplified by *Flower of Scotland* and the enthusiasm of the nation.

Our population is around ten times smaller than England so you've got to be competitive to succeed. There's a national fervour in Scotland which I've only seen once elsewhere in football. It was in the World Cup in Korea. I was working for the BBC in Seoul and everyone in Korea was wearing the team's red jersey for a month, from kids to grandmothers. That support reminded me of Scotland.

Of course it is balanced by the anti-hero thing too. You are not allowed to be too good at anything in Scotland. Anyone who gets too much success needs to be brought down a peg or two. It keeps your feet on the ground. I remember doing school visits as Scotland manager where a kid would ask for an autograph, then another and a third would say: "Who's he anyway?" That is definitely going to keep your feet on the ground. In Scotland we are all Jock Tamson's bairns – a group of people united by a common sentiment.

The great Bill Shankly influenced me a lot. I played for his brother Bob for six years at Dundee and they were very alike. Bill was a master at sports psychology – for example, the little things he did at Liverpool with his great 1960s side. In those days the teams never used to run out side-by-side like they do nowadays. Bill would

---

" My proudest moment is managing the Scottish team

send out his lads last and make the other team wait so they were underdogs before they started. And when the players got off the team bus he always sent big Ron Yeats first so people would say: "Christ, look at the size of them."

I remember when Bob Shankly used to position us for the team photograph. If you were a good player you were sat right in the middle of the picture. As you got out to the sides it was always a worry, and if you were positioned on the end you knew your days were numbered. "A simple pair of scissors will get rid of you, son," he would say.

My favourite player, who sadly died in March 2015, was Dave Mackay. He was so Scottish: tough, talented, uncompromising and ruthless. He was hard but never dirty. And when it was all over he would shake your hand and smile.

"I lived in Prestwick and Ayr for a while and I have two sons and a daughter who still live there. I really love the Ayrshire coast and the links golf courses: Turnberry, Royal Troon and Prestwick where the first Open was played."
Golfers at Turnberry

JACK BRUCE 1943-2014
bass guitarist and songwriter

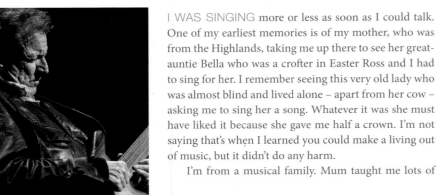

I WAS SINGING more or less as soon as I could talk. One of my earliest memories is of my mother, who was from the Highlands, taking me up there to see her great-auntie Bella who was a crofter in Easter Ross and I had to sing for her. I remember seeing this very old lady who was almost blind and lived alone – apart from her cow – asking me to sing her a song. Whatever it was she must have liked it because she gave me half a crown. I'm not saying that's when I learned you could make a living out of music, but it didn't do any harm.

I'm from a musical family. Mum taught me lots of Scottish songs, including Robert Burns's songs, which I still love, and I occasionally do them in concerts. My father played the piano and mandolin, my brother was a great piano player and my mother used to sing. Musically, it was a fantastic family to grow up in.

But I'd have been a factory worker if my father had had his way. Mum was all for me making a life for myself in music but my father said I should get a proper job and become an apprentice in a factory: a safe job. The factory later closed so I reckon I made the right decision!

I can understand why my father felt that way, though, as things had been hard for us in those post-war years near Glasgow, with quite a lot of upheaval. I was born in a mining area of Lanarkshire but then we moved to Canada for a couple of years, then we came back to Glasgow. Life was a struggle for my parents, trying to get their lives back on track in Scotland.

It was quite hard for me too. I went to lots of different schools and it was difficult to make friends, with all the moving around. In those days things were hard, not just where we were but in other parts of Britain too.

Still, there were some really great times as well –

As founder member of the supergroup Cream, Jack has been a global name in the world of music since the 1960s. Pink Floyd's Roger Waters described him as "probably the most musically-gifted bass player there has ever been." Jack released his final album Silver Rails in 2014. This was one of his final interviews before his death.

Cream: Jack (centre) with Ginger Baker (left) and Eric Clapton (right)

Jack in full flow in 1972

32

"I remember one Easter cycling round the mountains between Glencoe and Rannoch Moor. One minute it was snowing and I was absolutely frozen, then the sun came out and I got sunburn on my arms."

and a lot of them revolved round my bike. As soon as I could I got a bike and I was off. At first I'd cycle to Loch Lomond with a couple of friends and, by the time I was 14, we were doing some phenomenal cycle rides all over Scotland. I remember one Easter cycling round the mountains between Glencoe and Rannoch Moor. One minute it was snowing and I was absolutely frozen but then the sun came out and I got sunburn on my arms. Fantastic. Four seasons in one day, as they say.

I think every Scot is proud of the Highlands, the mountains, the views – it's all part of our heritage. I've always loved the west coast and my favourite place is Wester Ross where I used to have a little cottage. Then you go further into Sutherland where it's more wild and just as beautiful.

Back home in Glasgow, though, all I wanted to do revolved round music. I remember even at primary school I had a teacher called Douglas Burnie who recognised my talent and went round to my house to speak to my parents about it.

I later got a scholarship to go to the Royal Scottish Academy of Music and Drama and that's where I learned to play the cello. I wanted to play double bass but I was too little. They said I should leave it a year but try the cello in the meantime. So there I was studying cello and composition and harmony. At the time the RSAMD seemed very grand – and it was very grand – and with that went a certain stuffiness: an old-fashioned, Victorian feel. It just wasn't for me, so I left at the age of 17 and hit the road. Recently, though, they gave me an honorary Doctorate of Music so that worked out all right in the end!

I might well have stayed in Scotland if it hadn't been for my absolute commitment to making a life in music. In those days you had to leave if you wanted to make it. It's not necessarily that way now, but it was then. Leaving Glasgow was very difficult – it's in the blood – but there wasn't any choice.

Jack with his family in Wester Ross

I still go back when I can. I love Scotland (although the weather doesn't love me; these days I need to be somewhere where it's warm). I consider myself a citizen of the world but Scotland is in my heart. If you're Scottish, you're Scottish and you never lose that. When I'm away I have this romantic view of it, then when I come back I remember the bloody-mindedness that characterises a lot of Scots, especially Glaswegians (probably including me), and I love that too. That's what drives us on.

If you look at the people who've really made a name for themselves you wouldn't call any of them shrinking violets. Alex Ferguson, for instance. He made it by doing things his way and he really cracked it; he's got it sussed. There are some excellent modern Scottish classical composers like James MacMillan as well as contemporary and folk musicians. Great writers too like Irvine Welsh. And I think the fact that we have Europe's first freedom fighter in William Wallace says it all.

jackbruce.com

GORDON BUCHANAN
wildlife photographer and film-maker

A childhood fan of the naturalist David Attenborough, Gordon has travelled the world to capture wildlife on film. He has made major contributions to a range of wildlife programmes including Big Cat Diary, Springwatch, Natural World *and* Lost Land. *His influential documentaries include* The Bear Family and Me *and* The Snow Wolf Family and Me.

I WAS A BIT OF A FERAL CHILD – or at least I led something of a feral life growing up on the Isle of Mull in the Inner Hebrides. The population is quite small – there are more sheep than people and there are more hills than buildings. When I was young I would roam around wherever I liked with no one watching over my shoulder asking what I was up to. I just about lived outdoors. I loved animals and could think of nothing I wanted more than to work with horses when I grew up – so it's no surprise really that I ended up doing what I do for a living. In some ways I've never grown up beyond the age of nine or ten.

I was actually born in Clydeside – in Alexandria in the Vale of Leven. My folks divorced when I was seven. There were four of us kids, and my mum took us to Mull where my grandparents had a caravan, leaving her friends and family behind, as she thought it would be safer for us all.

For me, Mull is like Scotland in miniature. There was quite a diversity of people living there, but there was no snobbery and everyone lived together quite harmoniously. It was a terrific community. If there was any social divide I certainly never felt it. The richest of the rich kids mixed with the poorest of the poor kids and it didn't matter whether you lived in a castle or a caravan. There was that spirit of tolerance and fairness that I think pervades the Scottish psyche.

I loved it there but I always wondered what else the world had to offer. I used to go down to Tobermory and gaze across the Sound of Mull. Looking out to sea it seemed there were limitless possibilities, but I never

Gordon with his bear family

"I used to go down Tobermory and gaze across the Sound of Mull. Looking out to sea it seemed there were limitless possibilities."

thought I would get the opportunity to travel. I had never really been on holiday other than to Mull! I wasn't the best example of a schoolboy and, when I reached my teens, I didn't know what would become of me. I didn't expect I'd go to university, and I didn't want a job in the fishing industry. All I knew is that I wanted to explore.

Things fell nicely for me when I was about 17. I was working in a local restaurant when I met Nick Gordon, the husband of the owner. He was a wildlife cameraman. I'd listen to his stories and thought his life sounded incredible. He'd been to places like Africa, South America, China and the Middle East. I'd never met anyone like him before. He was windswept and interesting and we just hit it off. When he gave me the chance to go with him to Sierra Leone as his assistant I jumped at the chance. So off we went for a one-and-a-half year project.

I had expected it to be all giraffes browsing on acacia trees, and gin and tonic at sundown but of course it was much grittier than that. I wasn't prepared for the poverty I'd see there or the homesickness I would feel. At that time the only way to keep in touch with home was writing letters – then waiting two months for a reply. It was a complete culture shock but I think it was the making of me. I learned about 80 per cent of what I know from Nick. I worked with him for five years and was devastated when he died ten years ago.

I love my work and feel privileged that I can make a living out of it. It's funny when I meet some of my old teachers and they can't reconcile the boy they knew who had no real interest in schoolwork with what I have made out of my life.

One of the most special things I've done was spending the summer in the Arctic with wild wolves. A lot of the time as a cameraman you try to be as unobtrusive as possible – you're an unseen observer – but that isn't possible in the Arctic as there's nowhere to hide. You have to forge some kind of relationship or bond with the animals and adapt your behaviour to the individuals in the group. There's something about that place and those

animals which is completely captivating. And that rufty-tufty life sleeping in tents and hiking on glaciers is right up my street – it's a bit like I lived as a child.

Still, it's always great to come home to my real family and re-connect with Scotland again. One of my favourite places is the Abernethy Forest in the Cairngorms. It's part of the old Caledonian pine forest. What I love about it is that it looks today more or less as it would have 5,000 years ago. It's completely magical and mystical, and my wife and children think so too.

When I'm away I play a lot of music but I've got it on 'shuffle' so I don't really choose what I'm listening to at a particular time – it's whatever comes on. But sometimes you hear something that takes your mind straight back home. This happened to me in Mumbai in India. There was a festival going on with fireworks in the middle of a three-lane highway and I heard the sound of drums which was almost identical to the noise and rhythm of the drums of a pipe band in Scotland. The snare drums and bass drums seem to me quintessentially Scottish, but there I was in India hearing something quite similar. I had to record it on my phone. That sound is the spirit of Scotland for me – uptight and regimented but powerful

and emotive all at the same time. It's a sound that signifies major events like the Highland Games or a festival and it's the loudest and most insistent sound around.

We Scots definitely have our own identity, but it's not enough just to think we're wonderful – we have to back it up. That's why I thought having a referendum on the future of Scotland was terrific. It was a case of people not simply accepting what the newspapers say or what the status quo is, but actively making a choice. People were empowered fundamentally to make a decision about their country's life. People had a political voice and they embraced the opportunity.

If you look down the history of the Scottish people they are not easily influenced. They resisted the Romans and they had long struggles with England over the years. Scottish identity may have seemed cloudy and murky at times but it was always there. In 2014 people showed they wanted a clear identity. They put a lot of thought into that vote. That's what we are – a nation of thinkers.

@gordonjbuchanan

"One of my favourite places is the Abernethy Forest in the Cairngorms. It's part of the old Caledonian pine forest. What I love about it is that it looks today more or less as it would have 5,000 years ago. It's completely magical and mystical."

39

EILIDH CHILD

athlete

A track and field athlete who specialises in the 400 metres hurdles, Eilidh represented Great Britain at the 2012 London Olympics. She took silver in the event at the Commonwealth Games in Glasgow in 2014 followed by gold at the European Championships in Zurich the same year. She set the Scottish record for the event in 2013.

ALL MY FAMILY ARE SPORTS-MAD so it's not surprising that this is what I've chosen to do with my life. My older sister is a hurdler and my brother plays football but we all started off with swimming, as my mum taught in the local pool in Kinross where I grew up.

The area is best known these days as the place where the huge music festival *T In The Park* is held, but for me it's still the little town where my dad was the local policeman and everybody knew everybody else. I remember sport being really important at my school, especially sports day. When I was the school sports champion it was a big deal. Getting that title made you feel special.

So swimming was something we all did competitively, but I was always fascinated by athletics. I loved watching track and field and I was glued to the Barcelona Olympics on the TV. It was a great era with some real British heroes like Colin Jackson and Sally Gunnell. Closer to home I always admired the Scottish sprinter Ian Mackie who was the first Briton to beat Linford Christie in the 100 metres for years. We run for the same club and I remember being so impressed seeing him on the track and at training sessions.

My family life had evolved around various sports, both playing and watching. Like lots of Scots, we love football. My family are all big Hearts supporters and we would watch them when we could. Then training and competing in events would take up most of our time. My mum and dad were like a taxi service, taking us from one place to another.

But if my school days were a time devoted to sport, I took my eye off the ball a bit when I went to university

Eilidh with her Commonwealth Games medal

in Edinburgh to study Physical Education. Although I was on a sports course I was at the stage of rebelling a bit against my background. I was only 17 and I wanted to go out and have a drink and enjoy myself – just be a normal student. Before, I hadn't felt as if I was missing out but I decided to enjoy the lifestyle in Edinburgh. Also, it wasn't so easy to keep up with my regime as it was when I was at home. There was no Mum or Dad to ferry me to training; I'd have to walk and take two buses. Then I'd have to sort out everything else – there were no meals waiting for me on the table!

But after a couple years I think I had got all that socialising out of my system. I realised I missed training, and being in shape and competitive. I had kept competing on and off but I was getting beaten by people I would have beaten before. Having been a successful competitor, then taking a step away from it made me appreciate what I had. I got my hunger for it back. I realised it wasn't the

end of the world if I missed a party. I graduated and kept on training. Things were going well and I decided to be a full-time athlete. Not going out on the town didn't feel like a sacrifice any more.

But the biggest sacrifice for me was leaving Scotland, my family and my fiancé Brian to work with my coach Malcolm Arnold in Bath. I wanted him to coach me enough to make that move, although I am the last person you would have thought would do that. I was sure I would get homesick and had it in my head that it would be a difficult thing to do, but I was made very welcome and it helped me grow up a lot. People are friendly where I live now, but friendly in a different way from Scotland. I would always stop and say hello to everyone and have a chat in Scotland, but it's not really the done thing here.

I'm always telling people they should visit Scotland. The further north you go there the more you love it. We always had dogs and we would have all of our family

holidays in Scotland and take the dogs with us. My dad is from Oban so we'd go there and also up to Inverness and different places around the Scottish Highlands. One of my very favourite areas is around the Kyle of Lochalsh and Lochcarron. The iconic view of Eilean Donan Castle is known all round the world, and for very good reason. I also love the island of Islay. It's where I got engaged in 2013 so it holds very happy memories for me.

The following year, 2014, was also a good year for me. We had the Commonwealth Games in Glasgow where I got a silver medal, then two weeks later I got gold in the European Championships. It's great to get medals – that's what we train for – but I'm actually prouder of handling all the attention that was on all of the Scottish athletes during the Commonwealth Games. There was the spotlight from the media on us – the interviews, cameras and TV coverage – and also all the pressure of performing in front of a home crowd and all the nervous expectation that went with it. Most of us weren't used to it, but I hope I conducted myself well.

My parents always impressed on me how important it is to be a good sportsman and to shake your fellow competitors' hands after an event. They weren't bothered whether we won, but they were bothered about how we conducted ourselves. They were sticklers for good manners. They weren't pushy parents at all; they just wanted to make sure we were happy. Every night they would be taking myself or my brother or my sisters to something but it never seemed to be a problem. It's something I look back on now and appreciate how much they helped us all without making a big deal of it. There are some great athletes around, but my family are my biggest inspiration.

@eilidhchild

"I love the island of Islay. It's where I got engaged so it holds very happy memories for me."

PAT CLINTON

boxer

After years of success as an amateur and a professional boxer, including boxing in the Olympics, Pat won the World Boxing Organisation's Flyweight Champion's title in 1992, beating Mexican Isidro Perez at Kelvin Hall in Glasgow. The world-beating 'boy from Croy' had 23 fights in his professional career, winning 20 – nine of them knockouts.

MY AMBITION WAS TO BE A JOCKEY but, at 7 stone 4lbs when I was a lad, I was told I was too heavy. So I went into boxing, which is probably what I was destined to do. My father had been a Scottish level amateur boxer and he used to run a boxing club in a local village. Some of my brothers went along and it was easy for me to follow suit.

Once I got started it turned out that I had a natural talent for the sport. It's in the blood. Sometimes you have to embrace what you're given. It's God's gift that you're dealt and you realise that's the direction your life is going to go.

It meant I was different from my friends from school. My father wouldn't let me play football in case I got injured and he made sure I understood from the start that, to get anywhere in the boxing world, you have to be disciplined. Then later when my mates would go out and do all those normal things like having a beer, I would be down at the gym. From the age of 14-21 my life was centred on a routine of one night at the gym, the next running on the roads. If you want to be successful you have to sacrifice something.

I started boxing at the age of seven and from very early on I wanted to be world champion. I expected it to happen. For me, it is what I was doing all that training for. Then my dad died when I was 16, which was devastating. I could have given up, but my brother took over the reins and I just carried on.

It sounds a bit of a rigid existence for a boy, but I had a very, very happy childhood. I was born in the mining town of Croy – where I still live now – and I went to Holy

Pat raises his arms in triumph

"It was very special to me, being able to fight for the world title in Kelvin Hall in Glasgow."

Cross Primary School in Croy, then St Maurice's High School in Cumbernauld. We were a big family. I had five older brothers, three older sisters and one younger sister and there were only 13 years between us all. It was a lot of fun growing up in my family – really great. My parents were both from big families, too, so I had lots of uncles, aunts and a tremendous amount of cousins.

When I was 21 I had to go to London to develop my career and I lived there for five years. I hate cities so it wasn't the happiest time for me, although I was doing well with my boxing. I prefer the countryside and I couldn't wait to get on a plane or the train and come back to Croy and all the people in the village. Most of my family are there. That's where my heart is and always was. Mining villages tend to be tight communities and the people love their music. There's one miners' song I love called *Oft in the Stilly Night*. Listening to it just breaks your heart.

It was very special to me, being able to fight for the world title in Kelvin Hall in Glasgow. I think I've got my manager Tommy Gilmour to thank for that. He was great for me, and he also manages the darts champion Gary Anderson. I don't think anyone has managed two world champions in such different disciplines before. He always said to me: "If you win a world title nobody can take it away from you. It's in the record books forever."

The atmosphere that night was tremendous, with the home crowd right behind me and willing me to victory. I couldn't wait for the bell to go. But it's a lonely game, boxing. You're up there on your own and nobody can do it for you. It's not like football where there are 11 of you and you can bring on a substitute if you get injured

" The atmosphere was tremendous with the home crowd willing me to victory

or tired. I remember I was tiring quite badly in the last couple of rounds and my brother Michael could see I needed something to keep me fighting hard. He showed me a picture of my dad and my son and that inspired me to win it for them as well as myself and my country.

It was an amazing night and undoubtedly one of the most unforgettable moments of my life. But it was also my job – par for the course, in a way. I did expect to take a world champion title at some stage, and it happened as I always thought it would. Winning the European title in 1990 as the first Scot in 74 years was very special too. But, as I say, it's a tough life with a lot of sacrifices and I've been happy working as a joiner since retiring from the sport. Boxing's a business that takes its toll. I'd been boxing all my life, and obviously getting injuries along the way: I've broken both of my hands five or six times. Keeping your weight down to 112lbs is also hard.

My proudest moment was the night my son Sean was born. Now he's grown up and a joiner like me. I didn't want him to have the life I had, spending 25 years concentrating on just one thing. Boxing took over my life. It brought great rewards but it means you miss out on other things. But the good memories will always stay with me.

Oft, in the Stilly Night
BY THOMAS MOORE 1779-1852

Oft, in the stilly night,
Ere slumber's chain has bound me,
Fond memory brings the light
Of other days around me;
The smiles, the tears,
Of boyhood's years,
The words of love then spoken;
The eyes that shone,
Now dimm'd and gone,
The cheerful hearts now broken!
Thus, in the stilly night,
Ere slumber's chain hath bound me,
Sad memory brings the light
Of other days around me.

When I remember all
The friends, so link'd together,
I've seen around me fall,
Like leaves in wintry weather;
I feel like one
Who treads alone
Some banquet-hall deserted,
Whose lights are fled,
Whose garlands dead,
And all but he departed!
Thus, in the stilly night,
Ere slumber's chain has bound me,
Sad memory brings the light
Of other days around me.

"I couldn't wait to get on a plane or the train and come back to Croy and all the people in the village. That's where my heart is and always was."
On a high plateau on the east side of Croy Hill, the Antonine Wall is the site of an ancient Roman fort

BRIAN COX CBE
actor

One of Scotland's most accomplished actors on stage and screen, Brian has had leading roles with the RSC and his numerous film credits include Rob Roy, Braveheart, L.I.E., The Escapist, Troy *and* The Bourne Supremacy. *He played the title role in BBC's* Bob Servant *filmed in his home area of Dundee and in 2015 starred in* Waiting for Godot *at the Edinburgh Royal Lyceum Theatre. He has been Rector of Dundee University since 2010.*

I'M A MICK MAC. Most of my family hail from Ireland, although some are from the Scottish Borders. Either way, I have Celtic blood in my veins. I'd like to think I've got the best of both worlds, and certainly the performing gene runs through both cultures. If there's a difference I think it's that the Irish find it hard to say 'no'. Part of my Scottishness is being able to say 'no' and knowing when to draw a line.

Maybe that element of sticking to your guns and being strong and determined comes from being a Dundonian. The people there have gone through all sorts of difficulties and have been written off more times than you can imagine, but they still bounce back. They're incredibly resilient. That's a useful trait to have in the acting world.

As far back as I can remember I have always been a bit of a performer. My dad used to make me sing songs when I was a little boy, which I enjoyed, and that ritual of performance became my solace when he died when I was just eight years old. Another influence was going to the pictures. There were so many cinemas in Dundee and I was fascinated with films.

It's just as well my acting career took off as my education was disastrous, and I was hopeless at sport. Fortunately acting was what I wanted to do and I was lucky that it worked out for me. A couple of teachers at school saw something in my character, some kind of potential, and gave me a lot of encouragement. So I left school at 15 and started at Dundee Rep, and it was from there that it all happened. I had a clear trajectory and everything sort of fell into being. It was weird and wonderful and I feel very blessed that I could do exactly what I wanted in my life. The desire was strong from an early age. There were a few encumbrances on the way, but you just have to get over them. One encumbrance was how things were at home. We were dirt poor – my mum was shockingly poor after my father died. On Fridays I used to go to the local fish and chip shop and get the scraps of batter that were left over. That would be our supper.

Despite those hardships I have an abiding affection for Dundee, and being made Rector of Dundee University is one of the things I'm most proud of. Me, who left school young and never went to university. Now I have five honorary doctorates! When you're from Dundee the first thing you become aware of is water – the sea, the River Tay and what they both represent. To me they opened up the rest of the world. The river was

Princes Street, Edinburgh

49

Brian by the River Clyde

the fundamentals of life and they have a strong sense of egalitarianism and anti-feudalism. I think I'm blessed to be Scottish, and as I get older I feel a stronger contact with those sentiments.

That history of thought is very strong in Edinburgh. It's a Hanoverian city, a haunting city and the place I think of as my spiritual home. I love it there. There is a powerful sense of intellectualism and creativity, and you just need to wander round places like the Royal Mile to feel it. There's a tombstone to the poet Robert Fergusson which was paid for by Robert Burns and later repaired and maintained by Robert Louis Stevenson. Edinburgh is full of that kind of history and those connections.

I love the dichotomy that exists at the core of Scotland – it's like a thread that links what we are. There's the Protestant work ethic and Presbyterianism on one hand, then the relative freedom of the Catholic side on the other. I love the idea of extremes, of characters being repressed and the internal feud that goes with it, the Jekyll and Hyde syndrome. Robert Louis Stevenson is one of the most inspirational of Scots and is recognised as such, but we also have contemporary inspirational and world-class people who don't always get the credit they deserve. Stanley Baxter, for instance, is a world-class actor but isn't as revered as he should be. Fulton Mackay is another acting hero of mine.

Apart from Edinburgh, there are many places in Scotland that have a lot of meaning for me: my home town of Dundee, of course, and also islands like Mull and Iona. One place that especially lives in my mind is Kinnoull Hill in Perth which I climbed with my dad less than a year before he died. You can see Dundee and Perth and the beauty of the isles from the top. I always feel that his spirit is there watching, waiting for me to come home.

something to be crossed, to see what's on the other side, to get away and to explore – but always to come back.

Living in the United States, it's the people of Dundee I miss as much as anything – in fact Scottish people as a whole. The Scots have a shared heritage and a culturalism that I think are unique. Our roots run deep and are long-lasting, however much time we may spend away.

Scottish people care about their country and what it means to them and they actively engage with it. That is borne out by the independence referendum in 2014 with its near 85 per cent turnout. But this is nothing new. The enlightenment period in Scotland – led by great people like Adam Smith, David Hume and Francis Hutcheson – has affected us all and still lives with us. People discuss

"One place that especially lives in my mind is Kinnoull Hill in Perth which I climbed with my dad less than a year before he died. You can see Dundee and Perth and the beauty of the isles from the top. I always feel that his spirit is there watching, waiting for me to come home."

51

CHRISTINE DE LUCA

poet, novelist and Edinburgh Makar

Christine De Luca, who writes in both English and Shetlandic, was appointed Edinburgh's Makar (poet laureate) in 2014. She has had over a dozen books published, mainly poetry, but also a novel and some children's stories. Her latest collection, Dat Trickster Sun *(Mariscat 2014), was shortlisted for the Michael Marks Poetry Pamphlet Prize. Her poems have been selected three times for the Best Scottish Poems of the Year in 2006, 2010 and 2013.*

I WAS BORN on the tiny island of Bressay, Shetland in April 1947 but, from age two, brought up in Waas (Walls) on the west side of Shetland.

My first 18 years were spent in Shetland. Until I was about eight we had no electricity but were fortunate to have piped water and sanitation as we lived in the schoolhouse. The school – Happyhansel – had the unusual asset of a croft which we worked; so with croft, peats and boat we had a very traditional upbringing. I consider myself very fortunate in that respect.

Highlights of the annual calendar were somewhat seasonal: in the long light of the summer months we had picnics, the annual regatta and agricultural show, playing in the burn and sea-fishing (as well as croft and peat work); as the nights drew in it was 'casting kale' at Hallowe'en (pilfering cabbages and throwing them in porches!), Guy Fawkes night, sledging and guizing at Christmas and New Year and parties. The guizing involved dressing up, disguising ourselves and calling on as many houses in the township as we could. Young adult guizers also did this; with music and dancing involved. We also sewed and knitted a lot and played cards. Often we had cousins to stay or went to stay at their homes, which was always exciting.

We almost always had holidays in Scotland, sometimes with relatives and friends (in Portlethen, Denny and Coldstream) but we often rented accommodation. Mum selected the destination – quite diverse places such as Kippford, Lower Largo, Tomintoul and Inversnaid. We merely touched along cities. I loved the journey south to Aberdeen on the steamer. We were full of expectation as we saw our car being lifted up in a sling and

Foula i da hömin – Foula in the gloaming

tied down on deck. Usually we were met by our good friends from Portlethen. There were trees, douce air, fairgrounds, more children to play with, theatres, and … TV! The sea was disappointingly no warmer for swimming than in Shetland.

I do think Scotland is special, but it would be a poor country that wasn't thought to be special by its inhabitants. I like its relatively small size and population. You feel you know it. There's enough consensus and homogeneity of purpose but enough variety of breath-taking landscape and culture. It has a colourful history and has had some famous sons and daughters. Its cities are all very different and characterful, its education is still quite good, it has absorbed waves of immigrants reasonably well – Jews, Italians, Poles, Chinese, Indians, Pakistanis, Poles again – and is the richer for it.

I think being a small nation can make us outward-looking; we realise there's so much more out there. We have to strive to play a part in the wider world. I am very devoted to Shetland and to the Shetland dialect – it is distinctive within Scotland and very expressive. It is not always easy to be taken seriously as a writer when one writes in a minority tongue. But I don't let that deter me.

I was brought up to question things: religion, science, politics, and to enjoy argument and discourse – but that may be a product of my home rather than my nation. I think we can be delightfully maudlin about Scotland at times! It does have a pull on us.

I am retired from my day job in education but am fully engaged as a writer. If I think about how my background has shaped my work I'd say, in both cases, it has instilled diligence, dependability, going the extra mile,

"Shetland and Orkney represent a love of 'home' – the history, distinctive culture, language, amazing landscapes, birds and the canny people."
St Ninian's Isle and tombolo

Scalloway sunset

doing things for the joy of it not for recompense or recognition, being prepared to lead if necessary, taking a risk with an idea. My parents both had a very strong sense of community effort and respect for the past we build on, and I feel these have been guiding principles in my life which I learned very young. They were both creative by inclination and encouraged creativity. They were also people of faith, but open-minded, rational and tolerant. These things too have coloured my attitudes and values.

Being from Scotland probably did have a bearing on my choice of career. I started off as a secondary school teacher – I think there is still a deep respect for education in Scotland. Long may it last! In terms of earning a living in education, I could only ever have been a public servant – I have no entrepreneurial or commercial skills at all. Is that a Scottish trait? I think immigrant groups are perhaps more entrepreneurial. But I will work hard and creatively at whatever task has to be done. I love working with other people. I don't think these are particularly Scottish traits. My Scottish background necessarily informs my writing. If I came from somewhere else, my writing would most probably be very different. As writers we are products of a culture and, in turn, feed into that culture. I enjoy that.

I have several favourite places in Scotland. To start with, Shetland and Orkney: they represent a love of 'home' – the history, distinctive culture, language, amazing landscapes, birds and the canny people. I also love the north-west Highlands: there are some of the most beautiful landscapes in Britain there – it's ancient, monumental. The Borders are special, too: contrasting rolling hills and fertile valleys. Lovely little towns, each proudly different.

I live in Edinburgh and feel very much at home. I've grown to love Edinburgh – it's a beautiful city architecturally, set off by a strong physical landscape with many fine green spaces. Its festivals are legendary. It is big enough to support a fine range of theatres, galleries, and commercial facilities but is compact enough to walk around. The bus service is great and the trams are elegant. So I'm at home there – but Shetland still wins.

I'd describe the people of Scotland as 'bonnie fighters', with a feisty, belligerent streak but a sense of fair play.

We're perhaps not as different from others in the UK as we like to think but maybe we have a stronger sense of social justice, equality, the common weal. We have a good sense of humour and are able to laugh at ourselves, but sometimes have a wee chip on the shoulder. I'd say we're reasonably friendly and welcoming. We're not very demonstrative but, conversely, rather emotional about things like football and politics. There's a lot of creativity in Scotland.

There are a few Scots who have influenced or inspired me: poets like Norman MacCaig and Iain Crichton Smith; politicians like Donald Dewar, John Smith, Jo Grimond, Margo MacDonald; people who have overcome adversity to shine like Dame Evelyn Glennie; Shetland teachers like John and Lawrence Graham; many good colleagues over the years – and my own parents.

Becoming a mother is my proudest moment: it ranks above any literary or career success.

I don't like music aimed at making us homesick – there's a lot of it about. I love traditional Shetland fiddle music. It takes me 'home' without any overly sentimental quality and makes me proud of being a Shetlander. There are far too many fantastic fiddlers – it would be invidious to pick one.

christinedeluca.co.uk

edinburghmakar.org.uk

"I've grown to love Edinburgh. It's a beautiful city architecturally, set off by a strong physical landscape with many fine green spaces."

BARBARA DICKSON OBE

singer and actress

I HAVE A FLAT IN EDINBURGH NEW TOWN and am longing to return permanently. That hopefully will happen within a couple of years. I just haven't been able to come in the past.

I was brought up in Dunfermline, Fife to an English mother from Liverpool and a Scots father from Dunfermline, but his people were from Penicuik, Midlothian.

My most vivid childhood memories of Scotland revolve around the rich culture of the country. Music and pre-1960s architecture and the social behaviour of the time have really stuck with me.

I had happy, safe childhood days in Fife and used to love trips to the seaside in the summer, all on the bus. We had a big family in the area, but at home there was just me and my brother Alastair. He is a fine sculptor who now lives in Toronto, Canada.

We never went on proper holidays when we were children as my parents couldn't afford to go. We didn't have a car either. We used to spend most of our holiday time when I was very young in Liverpool with my mother's sister who was a railway cleaner at Edge Hill Station, a big junction there. I am very proud of my Liverpool roots as well as my Scots roots.

Scotland has its own identity and I love it dearly. It's full of colour and texture. I have lots of favourite places and landmarks. I love castles and particularly ruined abbeys and pre-Reformation buildings. Perfection for me is Melrose Abbey, Glasgow Cathedral and Falkland Palace, but most special is the Abbey Church in Dunfermline – Queen Margaret's church with its Romanesque nave.

I think the people of Scotland are special too. The

Falkland Palace in Cupar, Fife

"I love castles, ruined abbeys and pre-Reformation buildings. Most special for me is the Abbey Church in Dunfermline with its Romanesque nave."

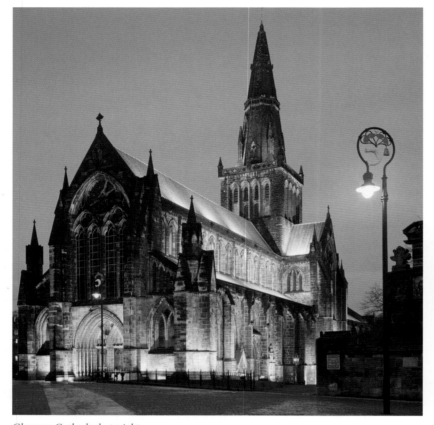

Glasgow Cathedral at night

Impressive architecture in Edinburgh New Town

folk on the east coast in the lowlands are very different from those in England, but they bear a resemblance to the people of Northumberland, which is logical, as the Lothians were part of the same country at one stage. We share the same DNA.

I'd describe Scots as phlegmatic, full of humour, straight-faced and straight-talking, but the character varies depending where you are in Scotland. Glasgow is unique in its own way. The people are very different from the Edinburgh folk and from people further north.

The Gaels have their own character too. This is all because the country is so big and sparsely populated.

When I think of the Scottish people who have influenced me, the list is almost endless. The main names that spring to mind are Robert Burns, Gerry Rafferty, Archie Fisher, Rab Noakes, Billy Connolly, Ian McCalman, John Byrne, John Bellany, James Robertson, John Watt, Lewis Grassic Gibbon, William Dalrymple, Michael Marra, Val McDermid, Iain Banks, Bill Bryden, Jimmy Reid, Hamish Henderson and Dick Gaughan.

I admire all of them and I'd also include Alexander McCall Smith – a great writer – too.

I have achieved an enormous amount in my career, but it's as nothing compared to my personal life and its towering moments. My marriage to my husband Oliver and giving birth to my three sons count as my proudest achievements. Oh, and getting the OBE from the Queen was fantastic. Very humbling.

barbaradickson.net

"Perfection for me is Melrose Abbey."

DONOVAN
musician

Born in 1946, Donovan Leitch celebrated 50 years in the music business in 2015. He was 18 when his single Catch the Wind *– which won the prestigious Ivor Novello Award – hit the charts. Pop star and folk troubadour Donovan was at the forefront of the 'flower power' generation and, as a keen follower of transcendental meditation as well as an accomplished musician, he was a major influence on* The Beatles.

I LOVED SEASIDE HOLIDAYS AS A CHILD. My Granny Kelly would take a wee 'but'n'ben' in Ayr each summer and we kids would huddle by the sea wall eating sang witches (as we called them) and riding the donkey on the dark, wide sands. After, when I'd gone to bed, Daddy would read me Lewis Carroll and I would dream of a sleepy yesterday of crinoline and parasol, bottled sand, and griffins dancing with dodos.

I was born in Maryhill in Glasgow and, at one year, moved to St Vincent Street, Anderston. Billy Connolly was born in Anderston, I think. My daddy was a photographer, mostly amateur but sometimes a pro at weddings and barmitzvahs.

The tenement where we lived had a comic book store across the tram-lines where I would buy *Superman*, *Supergirl*, *The Green Lantern* and *Mandrake The Magician* comics. I would lie awake and watch the trams' lights move across the ceiling of the old front room that

---

❝ I live in Scotland in my heart

I slept in alone. There were also parties in a room above the street and I heard the Scots and Irish songs which – although I didn't know it then – were called folk songs.

My proudest moment was when 20,000 souls were silent in Madison Square Garden as I sang my song *Isle of Islay*, solo on one acoustic guitar. But my favourite song that reminds me of my homeland is *The Great Silkie of Sule Skerry*. This is the tale of the Seal People of the Western Isles. A Seal Man lies with a human girl and a

"Roving the cliff, when fancy takes, felt like a tide left me here": from Donovan's Isle of Islay *which he sang at Madison Square Garden*

"My Granny Kelly would take a wee 'but'n'ben' in Ayr each summer and we kids would huddle by the sea wall eating sang witches (as we called them) and riding the donkey on the dark, wide sands."
The beach at Ayr

child is born, and one day out in the boat his Seal Father surfaces and meets his child.

I learned rhetoric from my father and he, in turn, from the great orators of the Scottish tradition. I remember he used to recite half hours of poetry in the bardic tradition, and his memory skills encouraged my own for my songs. I am the leading songwriter of the Gaelic tradition reaching all around the world with my compositions and performance in the ancient forms of bardic and troubadour skill.

Scotia – and that includes Gaelic Ireland as one tradition, not two – is so important in literature, music and social communications worldwide. Ancient knowledge is preserved in our Gaelic kingdoms which the Romans did not influence. Three million Scots and Irish entered America and, we now know, created for the most part the popular music we now enjoy. And, of course, Scotland invented the modern world.

I live in Scotland in my heart. Glasgow is my hometown and also my favourite city. The talent exploding there now is impressive and in one day there were four articles on the modern Glasgow creative drive in *The New York Times*.

Besides Sean Connery, the Scottish people who have most inspired me are Robert Burns and Robert Service – I remember my daddy used to read me their poetry.

The fact of the well-read Scot is well known. The people of Scotland are Gaelic wonders. In the 1700s travellers in Scotland reported that Scotia had the most educated populace of any European nation.

This I see as coming from John Knox who insisted each village have a teacher and that the Bible be read by all. Knox did not reckon on the other books being taught like Greek classics, democratic humanist and social teachings that have formed the Scottish educational system which is world-renowned. And we all know Robert Burns went to a village school that Knox began. The working man had a library, and so did my daddy ... and I have those books in my library now.

donovan.ie

@donovanofficial

"Glasgow is my hometown and also my favourite city. The talent exploding now in Glasgow is impressive."
The 'Armadillo' in the SECC complex in Glasgow

KAREN DUNBAR

comedienne, actress

After appearing in BBC Scotland's sketch show Chewin' the Fat *with Ford Kiernan and Greg Hemphill, Karen went on to star in* The Karen Dunbar Show. *She has played a range of roles on stage in Scotland and London's West End. She was lead compère at the Commonwealth Games in Glasgow in 2014 alongside John Barrowman.*

MY PROUDEST MOMENT was performing at a wee charity night in Ayr about 15 years ago with my dad in the front row. After the gig people were coming up and saying how much they enjoyed it. So I asked Dad what he thought. He smiled very genuinely and said: "Aye – good, hen." That was a huge compliment coming from him. I want to say I'm most proud of opening the Commonwealth Games which was a brilliant experience, but really it was that night in Ayr.

I was born in Glasgow and brought up in Ayr. I've been back in Glasgow since 1992 so I've lived half my life in each place. When I think back to my childhood in Ayr everything seemed sunny. It's a laugh when you think about it, but for some reason it seemed a lot hotter in the 1970s. I had many days down the beach and playing in Craigie Woods. The majority of my childhood was spent outside playing with my pals. Remember outside?

Holidays in those days involved regular trips to Grangemouth to visit family.

I was always a bit feart of Grangemouth! I think I was actually a bit scared of my nana. She was an amazing woman, really gregarious and charismatic, a real Scotch matriarch. She held court beautifully while the rest of the family tended her – and rightly so!

For me, Scotland is uniquely special in many ways. Its scenery is matchless, the depth of colours in the nature of Scotland takes my breath away. The people (us!) are a heady mix of warmth and straightforwardness. And our history is both tragic and heroic. I think we're a rare breed.

Being born and bred in Scotland has definitely helped make me the person I am. It's given me many useful traits. It's made me hard yet reasonable, canny and kind. It's given me deep humour and empathy. As a people I'd say we are honest, sturdy, warm, kind, rough, self-effacing, inventive and canny. I think those are the ingredients of our DNA.

I believe my background shapes the way I do my job at a depth I don't even think I'm fully aware of. The comedy that comes out of the experience of being brought up Scottish working class is limitless (just ask Billy Connolly) and I just love retelling funny stories about my upbringing and dramas and traumas of the people who so kindly – but firmly – nurtured me as a child.

Being from Scotland has helped me, not just in the richness of characters I've been able to imitate but also in the work ethic I was raised with. I've got the impression that we Scots have always had to work a bit harder to be just equal, and actually I think that's what makes us so successful.

There are plenty of Scots who I would say have influenced and inspired me down the years. The first one that comes to mind is Billy Connolly – a million times over. Also Elaine C. Smith because she was the first Scotswoman I saw being funny and successful. I like the writer Denise Mina for her smart and colourful wit and global appeal, and Lena Martell who was famous for singing *One Day At A Time*.

Everyone has their favourite places in Scotland. I love Ayr beach. I've got so many memories over decades of that strip of sand. I love the top north coast of Scotland. The shores are so pure and white and the sea's a heavenly bright blue colour. And there's a wee patch of stony coast just before you hit Port Glasgow that is an

"I was always a bit feart of Grangemouth!"

"I love Ayr beach. I've got so many memories over decades of that strip of sand."

Karen compèring the Glasgow Commonwealth Games ceremony with John Barrowman

especially precious place for me. If I could live anywhere in Scotland I'd probably build a wee croft on the cliff edge at Dunure and give the elements a run for their money.

There are a few songs and pieces of music that always remind me of Scotland, but if I had to narrow it down to one, I'd pick *The Fairy Lullaby* performed by Jean Redpath. My mum sang it to me as a baby and I still fill up whenever I hear it.

karendunbar.co.uk

@karendunbar147

"If I could live anywhere in Scotland I'd probably build a wee croft on the cliff edge at Dunure and give the elements a run for their money."
Dunure Castle

FISH
musician, actor, writer

Fish was frontman for the band Marillion which he joined in 1981. Its most successful album, Misplaced Childhood, *was number 1 in the UK charts for 41 weeks in 1985. He left two years later to go solo. Fish – real name Derek Dick – is widely acclaimed as a lyricist as well as a vocalist. He is also an actor and has appeared in both the* Rebus *and* Taggart *TV series.*

I BECAME VERY AWARE OF BEING SCOTTISH at the height of the Thatcher years in the 1980s when I was with Marillion. As a band we favoured going on writing retreats to get material together and we went to a castle in the Highlands, deep in berry-picking country, to work on our *Clutching at Straws* album. There was a strong sense of injustice in the UK, and especially Scotland, at the time. The poll tax was about to be launched in Scotland and it was a very serious issue. I suddenly felt Scottish again and started to be more political in my life. Not long after, I decided to leave Marillion and move back home.

I'd been living in the south of England during my time with Marillion. We had huge success – which most bands crave, I know – but we were just becoming like a huge machine that was taking us over. I'm a socialist and I was disillusioned with the music business whose core hierarchy isn't in the least socialist – it can be brutally corporate. It wasn't sympathetic to spirituality at all.

And coming back to Scotland was a spiritual thing for me. I wanted to get away from London and the music industry. I had lost my roots a bit and I wanted to re-establish and restablise myself. It was about my soul. I needed somewhere where I could have a rehearsal room, somewhere I could write and record, and I found a farmhouse in Haddington, East Lothian – the perfect place. I'd known Haddington since I was kid and it was as beautiful as I remembered it. I've been here ever since.

I was born in a hospital in Edinburgh and was brought up in Dalkeith where my father had a garage business. It was a nice place to grow up because it was in

A woodland path in the John Muir Country Park

the countryside but still near Edinburgh, on the perimeter of the big city. I had quite a middle-class upbringing but I wasn't privately educated – I went to Dalkeith High School. It was interesting because a lot of the land around was agricultural but there was also a mining industry in the area. At school some of the kids' dads were miners and there was a great sense of community.

When I left school I didn't go to university, although I did think about studying archaeology. I had always been interested in military history and nearly joined the Army, but I didn't do that either. I had no idea what to do with my life, really, but somehow I moved from the idea of going to college to doing an HND in forestry in the north-east of Scotland near Elgin. I worked in

"*I used to do a lot of scuba-diving, and St Abbs just north of Eyemouth on the east coast is a good spot for that. All down that coast there are beautiful beaches with spectacular hills to the west.*"
St Abbs

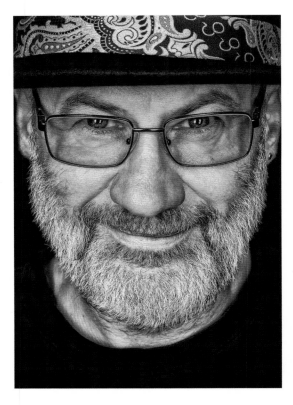

The song that reminds me most of Scotland is *Caledonia* – I hear it and I just howl

with a Geordie guitarist called Frank Usher. I remember doing my first gig in the Golden Lion in Galashiels. That led to me joining Marillion and moving south. I lived in different places – Aylesbury, Gerrards Cross and London – but I'd still come home between tours to see my family who had moved to North Berwick.

Music, acting and, more recently, writing have been my work for many years, although I never really made a conscious decision about making a living out of any of them. But there are a few different elements about my background that I think have had a bearing on what I've done in life. I was brought up around story-telling when I was a kid. And living in a community where everyone connected and where there was friendliness and openness – coupled with that Scottish sense of injustice – have helped me develop. Recently things like Facebook and writing blogs have really inspired me to make a change, and I think I will soon leave behind the music business and concentrate on writing.

So my music career will be behind me soon enough, and there'll be more changes as I'll be living in Germany, but Scotland will never leave me. Germany is fantastic and I won't be short of woodland or forest to visit, but if there's one thing I'll miss it's the sea and the coastline. I used to do a lot of scuba-diving, and St Abbs just north

of Eyemouth on the east coast is a good spot for that. All down that coast there are beautiful beaches with spectacular hills to the west. Yellowcraig is one of the best. John Muir Country Park in Dunbar is another of my favourite places.

Having been brought up near Edinburgh, the city has especially good memories for me. It's one of the most beautiful cities in the world and I love the vibe there. I used to enjoy hanging out at places like the Café Royal and doing a bit of writing while I was there. Nowadays the creatives gravitate more to Glasgow – it's probably got more of an artistic vibe for up-and-coming creative people; it's more of a melting pot.

The Pentland Hills to the west of Edinburgh are spectacular and I've also got a place in my heart for Elgin and Lossiemouth between Inverness and Aberdeen where I used to work as a forester.

The song that reminds me most of Scotland is *Caledonia*. Sometimes I hear it and I just howl. I recorded a version of it as a tribute to Frankie Miller whose version everyone knows. I had the pleasure of his company a few times over the years and love his strong independence and maverick attitude. Although he never wrote *Caledonia* he made it his own and I was privileged to be asked to sing it on his tribute album. Frankie was in the studio when we recorded it and it gave me an immense sense of relief when he congratulated me on the performance.

fishheadsclub.com

Speymouth forest and I loved it up there. Then I went to Germany for the first time and it had a profound effect on me and would do for the rest of my life. Now I'm planning to move to Germany to be with my partner and her family. But back then I returned to Scotland and went to live in the borders near Selkirk.

I'd never really considered music as a career, but I joined up with a band called Blewitt in 1980, working

"Edinburgh has especially good memories for me. It's one of the most beautiful cities in the world and I love the vibe there. I used to enjoy hanging out at places like the Café Royal and doing a bit of writing."

71

LAURA FRASER

actress

Trained at the Royal Scottish Academy of Music and Drama, Laura's first big break was in the BBC series Neverwhere *at the age of 19. Following numerous appearances in both British and American films and TV series and shows, she took the role of Lydia Rodarte-Quayle in the ground-breaking and highly acclaimed US crime drama* Breaking Bad.

WE'VE MOVED BACK to the West End of Glasgow where I was born and brought up after many years away.

I lived in Scotland until I was 19, then I moved to London to play the part of Door in Neil Gaiman's *Neverwhere* for the BBC. After London came Ireland and later New York: for a while up to the summer of 2015 we lived upstate New York in the woods. But I missed my family and friends and Glasgow itself, and I wanted my daughter Lila to go to school there.

I remember really long summers playing outside all over the West End of Glasgow. It felt like we had the full scope of the city but in reality it was probably just a few back gardens and parks! I would follow my big brother Kyle everywhere when I was wee. We would be on the move all day, riding our bikes and climbing walls and trees and scrambling over and under things.

Our back garden connected with lots of our neighbours' gardens and I remember all of the kids putting on shows every summer. They were sort of variety shows, although occasionally there was a narrative that I think probably only made sense to the kids! You would be out and about with no sense of time as it seemed endlessly bright and another kid would tell you that your mum was looking for you and that meant it was time to go home and get your dinner and go to bed.

One of my favourite places in Glasgow is The Kibble Palace in The Botanic Gardens. As a kid it felt so luxurious to go to this giant palace made of glass that was warm and full to the brim of spectacular plants and flowers from all over the world.

Even on a dull day the cloudy glass softens the light and makes it bright and sparkly inside. I always wished

The Kibble Palace in The Botanic Gardens

"One of my favourite places in Glasgow is The Kibble Palace in The Botanic Gardens. As a kid it felt so luxurious to go to this giant palace made of glass that was warm and full to the brim of spectacular plants and flowers from all over the world."

one day that I could get married inside the Kibble Palace! I like to bring my daughter there to walk around and be cosy on a cold day and look at the beautiful old marble sculptures dotted in between the plants.

Another of my favourite places is Kelvingrove Art Gallery. We used to go there on rainy Sundays. I loved wandering around such a beautiful building, with quiet stone staircases all to yourself and marble floor as far as your eyes could see. Nobody ever seemed to tell you off for exploring, so it felt like it belonged to us a little bit. I liked looking at the old paintings and imagining how people used to live. There used to be a glass beehive that connected to the outside through a transparent tube. I used to stare at that in total fascination. I worried that the glass would crack open and the bees would all swarm out at us, but that just made it more exciting to stand so close!

We used to eat a ham sandwich in the cafe afterwards, and maybe a fern cake. Then sometimes we would go across the road to the helter skelter park which is no longer there. We used to run about like mad on this huge metal structure full of chutes and poles and passageways. It was graffitied and noisy and wild and I loved banging along the metal tunnels with the other kids.

I love Glasgow, and find it so beautiful. The architecture there is stunning, and it's hard to choose only a few of my favourite places as I love so much of the city.

I don't think my accent has changed that much even though I've spent a long time away from Scotland. As an actor, I think I've only used my natural Scottish accent a handful of times whilst filming. At first I was doing a lot of English accents, and a few different European accents. Lately I have been doing a lot of American accents, like playing Lydia in *Breaking Bad*. Actually Vince Gilligan, the creator of *Breaking Bad*, came over to Edinburgh in 2013 for a brief visit. He was being interviewed as part of the Edinburgh Film Festival I think. It's always such a treat when I play a character who is Scottish as it feels a lot more free for me to work in my own accent.

It's lovely when you hear of other Scottish people doing well in the world. I get a kick out of hearing a Scottish band on the radio when I'm out of the UK. I love the song *Mother Glasgow* as sung by Hue and Cry. I cry my eyes out if I hear that song when I'm homesick! It tells such a moving story. I love the line 'Mother Glasgow watches all her weans...trying hard to feed her little starlings, unconsciously she clips their little wings'.

Scotland has produced so many people who have inspired me. These include Annie Lennox, Eddi Reader, Billy Connolly, Karen Dunbar, Tilda Swinton and Elaine C. Smith to name a few, but there are many, many more.

"On rainy Sundays I loved wandering around Kelvingrove Art Gallery – such a beautiful building, with quiet stone staircases all to yourself and marble floor as far as your eyes could see."

KATHERINE GRAINGER CBE

rower

Katherine is Britain's most successful female rower. She won Olympic gold in the double sculls with Anna Watkins at London 2012, adding to her silver medals from Sydney in 2000, Athens in 2004 and Beijing in 2008. She also has six world championship titles in her collection. She is Great Britain's most decorated female Olympian alongside the swimmer Rebecca Adlington.

MY SPORTING JOURNEY began not in a boat but in a sports hall when my secondary school art teacher Mr Davis started a lunchtime karate class. It taught me a great deal about mental discipline, determination, patience and perseverance as well as coordination and balance – all core lessons which helped me when I later took up rowing. By the time I left school I had achieved my black belt under Ken Davis's wonderful guidance and I gained a huge respect for sport as well as for fellow athletes.

I was born and bred in Glasgow. My family had moved to Bearsden literally days before I was born. I arrived a little earlier than planned, I should add, given that my parents had not had time to check the quickest way to the hospital and I was very nearly born somewhere on the road between Bearsden and the Queen Mother's Maternity Hospital in Glasgow!

I have very happy memories of growing up just outside Glasgow. I have a big sister who was just a year older than me in school years and we were very lucky where we lived in that there were loads of kids in our street who were the same age as us. Every evening everyone would gather in the cul-de-sac behind our house and play hide and seek, football, ride bikes. Back then it felt as if the long summer evenings went on forever. I've always found Glasgow a very friendly and vibrant place and as I grew up I loved trips into the city for concerts. When I was growing up it was the time of Texas, Deacon Blue, Simple Minds and Wet Wet Wet. Nowadays, however, the song which probably reminds me most of Scotland is the Proclaimers' *500 Miles* from many singalong nights, and of course it was also the adopted anthem of the Glasgow Commonwealth Games 2014. I also love any ceilidh music for all the celidhs I've ever danced at – and there have been many!

All my early holidays were in Aberdeen where my beloved gran and grandad lived. My sister and I were spoilt rotten by them and we absolutely loved going to visit. We always spent time on Aberdeen beach running in and out of the freezing cold sea, screaming as the shock of the waves hit us, and then being warmed by huge beach towels and eating picnics that Gran made up, including her own delicious home-baking. My long-suffering grandad would do anything for us and we repeatedly dragged him around the funfair at the beach.

Scotland has a wonderful sense of space and peace and is also a country of stunning contrasts. The cities are very cosmopolitan and dynamic yet the mountains and lochs have a breathtaking remote rugged beauty to them. Scotland made me the person I am, with an appreciation of family and home as well as giving me drive and resolve, while always retaining a sense of humour and fun. All typical Scottish characteristics.

I fell into rowing at Edinburgh University when I was studying for my law degree. I was lucky to have learned to row at university where I had a visionary coach, Hamish Burrell, who had a huge influence on my career. He believed in me and supported me from novice student rower to being a full member of the Great Britain squad. I didn't ever expect to be a full-time athlete. Initially it wasn't the sport that hooked me – it was the people. I have always had the enormous good luck to row with some of the most talented, inspiring, charismatic, engaging, fun people and I loved being in the team. After a few

"Edinburgh Castle where, for many a Hogmanay, I watched fireworks cascade down the side of it."

years I was encouraged to go to Great Britain trials and never looked back from that point onwards. My proudest moment was the Olympics in London 2012. After three previous Olympics where I had won silver medals, I finally achieved my dream gold medal which was even more incredible than I could possibly imagine with a home crowd supporting us down the rowing course.

There have been quite a few inspirational people in my life. At Edinburgh University there was a student called Dot Blackie a few years before me. Her picture was up in the boathouse and I remember being in awe of her as she had been the first female Boat Club Captain and had gone on to the Olympic Games. She was inspirational and helped me to believe the journey to the top was possible. A few years later I went to my first Olympic Games in the same team as Dot.

I was also very lucky to have the author Alexander McCall Smith as one of my law lecturers. He was a wonderful, humorous and impressive lecturer, retaining an amazing passion for teaching and the law. It's been great to see him become such a fantastic success in the literary world too. But I'd say my family definitely had the biggest and strongest effect on my life. They influenced and inspired me, and continue to do so every day.

The people of Scotland are fun, self-deprecating, generous, talkative, friendly, tough, strong, creative, honest, patriotic, feisty, sociable, bold, hard-working and sentimental. I don't currently live there as my job as a full-time member of the GB Rowing team is based elsewhere but I will always consider moving back.

I have many, many favourite places such as Edinburgh Old College because that's where I was a law student and it is a suitably impressive, inspiring building. I love Edinburgh Castle where, for many a Hogmanay, I watched fireworks cascade down the side of it. Aberdeen Castlegate is a special place as it's where my gran volunteered for decades in a charity shop and is now the home of my gold post box, and Aberdeen beach holds some of my happiest childhood memories. The Finnieston crane by the Clyde in Glasgow somehow always symbolises Scotland. Cameron House on the banks of Loch Lomond has beauty and tranquillity. And finally I'd mention the Kelvingrove Art Gallery and Museum in Glasgow where I learnt about everything from Egyptians to dinosaurs and Charles Rennie Mackintosh to Claude Monet.

Happy memories indeed!

katherinegrainger.com

"The Finnieston crane by the Clyde in Glasgow somehow always symbolises Scotland."

JOHN GREIG MBE
footballer, manager, director

Having devoted his entire footballing career as player, captain, manager and director to Rangers Football Club, John was voted the greatest ever Ranger in 1999. He won three domestic trebles and lifted the European Cup Winners' Cup in 1972 as captain. He is now Rangers' honorary life president. He also captained the Scotland team and was awarded the MBE in 1977.

I HAD NEVER SEEN A TELLY before I was ten. I didn't even know what one was. The nearest I had come to anything like that was listening to boxing matches on the radio with my father. That changed one Saturday afternoon when I was playing outside and a lady who lived near us shouted at me from the top floor to go up to her door. I thought she must have wanted me to go to the shops for a message for her, but instead she asked me in, sat me down on the floor and gave me a biscuit and a glass of lemonade. Then she went towards this box in the room and it lit up and there was the FA Cup final between Bolton Wanderers and Blackpool – the famous Stanley Matthews final, as it later became known. I remember that so clearly.

I was born in 1942 and brought up in Edinburgh, the youngest of six children. I was a late baby and there were nearly 20 years between me and my next oldest brother Tom. When I was little it was the end of war and times were tough for a lot of people. Things were tight but there was a strong community spirit and we all supported each other and enjoyed each other's company.

We lived in a tenement and I used to spend all my time kicking a tennis ball around in the street. There weren't many cars on the road so it was safe. I probably got more enjoyment out of that than children with their fancy machines that they play with nowadays. A lot of my first and happiest memories are from that time. Youngsters from the houses around would all be outside together and people would lean out of their front windows and watch us. Our only concern was keeping an eye out for the policeman on the beat and the people

whose gardens we'd trample on as we dashed in and out of them to retrieve the ball.

The first inkling that I might go somewhere with football was in the school playground at the age of about nine-and-a-half. I was running after the ball with the other kids as usual, when a teacher called me into a classroom and said he had been watching me and that I should go to school trials. I did, and they wanted me to play in the Edinburgh Schoolboys Cup final, but I didn't have any boots. So they opened up this cupboard and it was full of boots – heavy, solid things, more like miners' boots compared to what footballers play in today. I took them home and my brother Tom took off the old studs and put new ones on and new laces for the match. I got my first ever medal, but sadly I had to give the boots back.

My next big match was against Leith Schoolboys at Easter Road. I scored two goals, and the Edinburgh Evening News dubbed me the second Bobby Johnstone – a Hibs player who was also small, as I was at the time. It didn't go down very well with my family who were all Hearts supporters! I was starting to draw attention from different clubs and I played a bit at Tynecastle. That built my hopes up, but Hearts didn't come in for me until it was too late.

It turned out a Rangers scout had been watching me. He came round to have a look at my brothers and sisters to see if they were small like me. They were all a fair size so it was obvious I wasn't always going to be small and I was asked to Ibrox to have a look around. Much of my life revolved around football and that was

"I love Edinburgh, walking round the Braid Hills and looking out over the castle and right out to the Firth of Forth. It's a beautiful sight."

all I ever wanted to do. I wasn't interested in going out socially as I never had much money in my pocket anyway.

My big moment came one Sunday morning. My father was up and about early and I had a feeling something was up, but I had no idea what. Then the scout from Rangers turned up. He gave me the whole spiel about Rangers and handed me a provisional form to sign up. I didn't want to but my father insisted. Afterwards I started to cry because I was a Hearts supporter and I wanted to play for them, but Tom told me to take my chance, that Rangers was a great club and I would never look back.

I went out to tell my pal John that I had signed for Rangers. He said they were playing against Hibs at Easter Road and so we went to see them. They beat Hibs 6-1 and I thought: "That's some team." Tom was right. From that moment on I never looked back.

This was November 1958 and I was an apprentice engineer. In those days you kept on your apprenticeship and trained with your club two nights a week. I did that for nine months, going back and forth between Edinburgh and Glasgow. A few months later on they asked me if I would like to go full-time.

At that time good players usually moved on to English clubs, but I never had any need to do that: I was at the best club in Scotland where I played for 18 years, and was captain for 13 years. Lifting the European Cup Winners' Cup was a big, big thing but I felt then as I do now – that it was a win for the supporters, not for any individual footballer. That was the third time we had been in a European final and the supporters deserved it.

It was an honour for me to be the team captain, following in the footsteps of some great captains, and I was privileged to manage the club for four-and-a-half years. When I was voted the greatest ever Ranger in 1999 and they put up a statue of me along with the names of the 66 people who died in the disaster in Ibrox in 1971 I was quite taken aback. But I felt it was fitting that there

should be something at the ground for the bereaved families to go to which paid tribute to those supporters who lost their lives. And after the disaster Ibrox was in the forefront of British football grounds as far as safety was concerned.

I have always been given a lot of respect by the Scottish public, and even some Celtic supporters ask to shake my hand. That's a great thing about our people. In turn, I was taught to give everyone the respect they deserved from the greatest man I ever met – Eric Gardener. He used to run the boys club where I played as a teenager and he wanted us not just to be good players but good people as well.

Your early days are always in your heart and I still love Edinburgh, walking round the Braid Hills and looking out over the castle and right out to the Firth of Forth. It's a beautiful sight. Coming from the east side of Scotland, I am still amazed at some of the places and the views there are in the west. It's a lovely country. If we had decent weather no one would ever leave!

The memorial statue at Ibrox

CLARE GROGAN

actress, singer, presenter, novelist

Rising to early fame in the film Gregory's Girl *alongside John Gordon Sinclair, Clare was also the lead singer of the band Altered Images whose hits included* Happy Birthday. *She has continued to act on stage, screen and for television series including* Red Dwarf. *Clare is a regular radio presenter and has also written a children's novel called* Tallulah and the Teenstars.

I WASN'T BLASÉ as a teenager, but all the things that happened to me – like being in a film and signing for a major record label – seemed almost normal at the time. I was just doing a hobby I was enthusiastic about. Now, when I look back, the thing I'm proudest of is not one particular role or job, but simply being able to keep going in one of the toughest businesses there is.

My parents were strict Catholics, but they neither encouraged nor discouraged me in my acting and dancing and singing. They just let it happen, which I think did me a favour. They trusted me to do the right thing, which would have made it hard for me to break their trust.

I was born in Glasgow and my mum, dad and big sisters Margaret and Kathleen lived in a tenement in the Garnet Hill area right beside the Glasgow School of Art. I do think Glasgow is a very cultural city and it was back then, even though it didn't really have that kind of reputation. It was probably a bit of a rough area where we lived, but I never noticed at the time. Hill Street, Glasgow was my whole world at the time, as the street where you live is when you are young. We moved to the south side of Glasgow when I was ten, but I still have a great affection for my first home. I actually revisited our old flat for a TV programme and it was lovely to see a young couple living there with their kids, just like us. Everything round there is a bit more yuppified now, though.

My first professional job was at the age of four, in a story-telling show on STV where a group of children sat at the feet of the story-teller, Lesley, and responded to her (in no doubt a cute fashion – we were all aged four or five). I had been chosen by a scout who came to my nursery school. I can only barely remember doing it but I think I liked the in-between snacks best! So I started young and just carried on.

There was always something in me that made me want to perform. I was quite shy, and one thing that helped me conquer that was pretending to be someone else. I loved an audience and making people laugh and I was the class clown at school. If I went to see a ballet I would come home and re-enact the whole thing – very badly!

I was in the Scottish Youth Theatre and was always out and about acting in something or going to music sessions. I'd get home from school, change out of my uniform and jump into a transit van to be whisked off somewhere. The part of Susan in *Gregory's Girl* came up, and off I went to do it. It was great to be in a film and get the chance to act, because that was my passion. But none of us really thought this would be the start

Clare in her days with Altered Images

"Kelvin Way in Glasgow is a lovely, sweeping boulevard with a beautiful park, art galleries and the university."

of something big – it just seemed like a fun thing to do. I certainly never thought I would still be talking about it 30 years later. I've talked to John Gordon Sinclair about it and he felt the same.

Around this time I joined Altered Images and went off travelling round the world. I was only 18 and it was an exciting time. Then I'd come back and be dropped off at home in a limo, and my parents would usher me into the kitchen to do my own washing. Their not being impressed by me kept my feet on the ground. That's probably a bit of a Scots attitude. For me, being Scottish was a big part of how I grew up and it made me what I am now. In Glasgow there's a strong sense of community and a real desire amongst its people to look out for each other – but they never let you get above yourself.

I think my Scots background has given me a determination and durability that has helped me keep going. I never had a plan, but when I found myself in a position where an opportunity came up, I would usually grab it. I never took anything for granted. You do one thing then it sends you off in another direction. I started being a presenter after I was in an interview about acting and I just started interviewing the interviewer! In this business when you're in your thirties you sometimes have to reinvent yourself and take what comes your way – you don't necessarily get to do it on your own terms.

It's worked out for me. I've kept working and kept motivated and have had great opportunities to do things like film shows and travel shows, and I've worked on *The One Show*. It's been lovely. Now, as a mum, I have to look at what jobs come up and it has to tick a few boxes for me to be able to do it. But I always put everything into whatever I'm asked to do. I have a really strong work ethic.

I love it when I get a chance to work in Scotland. My dad and one of my sisters are there and my husband's family are too so, although we live in London, we go back to visit a lot. Whenever people ask me what is the one place they should go to in Scotland I tell them to take a daytime walk on Kelvin Way in Glasgow. It's a lovely, sweeping boulevard with a beautiful park, art galleries and the university. And, maybe because we used to live so close to it, one of my favourite places is the Glasgow School of Art, where my niece goes now. I love the work of Charles Rennie Mackintosh who designed it and I'm looking forward to seeing it restored to its former glory after the fire. It will rise from the ashes.

The piece of music which always reminds me of Scotland is *Happiness* by The Blue Nile. It takes me right back to something that I love – pop in the 1980s.

@claregrogan2

*"One of my favourite places is the Glasgow School of Art.
It will rise from the ashes."*

CAT HARVEY
broadcaster, performer, writer

Cat started her career as a sports reporter for the Evening Times newspaper and Scottish television. She was an award-winning presenter on Real Radio, has appeared in several pantomimes and has a regular column in the Sunday Mail newspaper. She wrote a book called The Cat's Whispers *about her time on Real Radio which she left in 2014 to concentrate on writing and theatre work.*

I STARTED OFF as a sports journalist and ended up as a pantomime fairy, so it's fair to say I've had a pretty varied career. I've done a lot of different things down the years, and I still don't know what I want to do when I grow up!

It was probably inevitable that I'd end up in the world of entertainment in one form or another, given my upbringing. My dad was a well-known fiddle player – he was a Scottish champion fiddler in the 1960s – and had his own band called the Bobby Harvey Ceilidh Band. They used to go on tour with a full-on Scottish show featuring Highland dancers, a singer and a piper as well as the band's own musicians. They would go all around the Clyde coast, and some of my earliest memories are of my brother and I being carted around in a camper van with the band.

We'd go to places like Largs, Rothesay and Millport and somehow both my brother and I would end up on stage – especially in Largs when the singer didn't come back from the pub. I'd sing songs like *You Cannae Shove your Grannie aff a Bus* and I was never fazed by having to do it. I was too wee to realise it was scary.

Even when the tours were over and we were back home in Milngavie the entertainment just continued. There were always parties going on, and everybody that came to the house would play an instrument or sing or recite a poem or do a turn of some sort. I just grew up with it all as part of normal family life. Dad also used to tour with the White Heather Club and apparently I was nearly born in Andy Stewart's house. My parents were there one evening and I nearly popped out. They managed

to get my mum to Yorkhill Hospital in Glasgow just in time, but I wish I'd been born at Andy's.

Rather than music though, sport was the big thing for me and this was where I wanted to work. I was borderline-obsessed with Partick Thistle at the age of 13, and I knew then that I wanted to be a sports journalist. My thinking at the time was that I could get into the football games without having to pay.

I did an MA in theatre, film and television at Glasgow University and a postgraduate degree in journalism at Stratchclyde. The day after I finished I started a job at the Evening Times as the first female football journalist in Scotland. You can imagine how that went down at the time. Sport was a very male-dominated part of the newspaper and you were expected to start at the bottom and work your way up, not just swan into a great job from the start. Although the sports editor was great it didn't go down very well with some of the others and I had to develop a thick skin. I compensated – probably overcompensated – by becoming obsessive about facts. As it happens, the players and the managers at the football clubs were fine with me once they realised that I knew my stuff.

After one and a half years I went to STV to present and report on sport and I stayed there for six years. One of the best things was presenting the highlights of the Champions League alongside Billy McNeill of the Lisbon Lions – the Celtic team who won the European Cup in 1967. He became like my surrogate dad. He's a wonderful man, an iconic Scottish player and one of Scottish football's absolute legends.

At the time it wasn't that common to have female sports presenters on TV either. Luckily Hazel Irvine had blazed the trail before me. When I had my first placement at the BBC she looked after me. She's an adorable person and was really happy to share her knowledge with me and help me along.

I had many happy years in radio, presenting on all sorts of different topics. I love presenting live events. One of the funniest was the Retrofest at Culzean Castle. It was a big 1980s festival with over 35,000 people. I presented from the stage on roller-boots and didn't injure myself, which was a result. I've been to nearly every T in the Park and got to interview most of the bands. It's nice to enjoy your work and win awards for it at the same time. I remember going to the Arqiva Commercial Radio Awards in London with my co-presenter Ewen Cameron who I'd worked with for a fantastic two years. There were paparazzi photographers outside and well-known broadcasters from all round the UK. Hardly anyone knew who we were. We walked in as if we were part of the waiting staff, then walked out with the biggest award of the night – UK Breakfast Show of the Year.

My broadcasting career has meant I've been able to travel all around Scotland. It's such a beautiful country and I love the places and the people. It makes me proud and patriotic: cut me in half and I'm tartan! I would rather holiday here than anywhere else.

Being from Milngavie I had the best of both worlds because we were just seven miles from Glasgow, with all the benefits of the big city like football, theatre and entertainment, but only two miles away from the

"Seil Island north-west of Oban has a particularly strong pull for me. My mum's auntie had a house there and every year that was where we'd go to spend our holidays. You have to cross Clachan Bridge to get there – an old stone bridge across the Atlantic."
Clachan Bridge

89

countryside, 20 minutes from Loch Lomond and near the West Highland Way. Everybody who lives in the area must do that walk – it's almost obligatory.

Some places have a particularly strong pull for me. One is Seil Island north-west of Oban. It's got so many connections for me. My mum was evacuated there during the war and went to primary school there. It's a quarriers' island with beautiful cottages. Mum would do her sums on slates. Her auntie had a house there and every year that was where we'd go to spend our holidays. We'd be dumped there in June and picked up in August. You have to cross Clachan Bridge to get there – an old stone bridge across the Atlantic.

The west coast where we travelled with Dad has great memories. One of the required things you just have to do is get the last sea-going paddle steamer called Waverley over to Rothesay. It's hilarious on a Saturday. You get people from every walk of life on those trips. The last time I did it there was a group of 30 women dressed as pirates, a 70th birthday party, an 18th birthday party and a stag do – everyone living it up together.

Then there's the outer Hebrides – probably the most beautiful place in the whole of Scotland. You go to any of the beaches on Harris and there's turquoise sea and golden sands to rival anything in the Caribbean – except with the Highlands in the background. You can find a beach in Harris and just about have it to yourself. It's picture-perfect.

Because of my dad I've always got songs in my head that evoke Scotland. I know most Scottish waltzes, jigs, strathspeys and reels. From my Tartan Army travels songs like *Loch Lomond* by Runrig, *Caledonia* by Dougie MacLean, Eddi Reader singing *Wild Mountainside* – and anything by Burns – bring a wee lump to my throat.

The West Highland Way

Being an old-fashioned soul I like a lot of Gaelic stuff. One of my favourite tunes that Dad used to perform has a bit of a morbid title – it's Niel Gow's *Lament for the Death of his Second Wife* – but I defy anyone to listen to it and not be moved. Dad used to say: "She must have been a cracker because he never wrote anything for the first one."

@misscatharvey

"One of the required things you just have to do is get the last sea-going paddle steamer called Waverley over to Rothesay on a Saturday sail. It's just wild. You get people from every walk of life living it up together."

ARMANDO IANNUCCI OBE
satirist, writer, director, producer

Armando Iannucci is best known as the writer of the Alan Partridge comedy TV series starring Steve Coogan. He rose quickly through BBC Scotland and Radio 4, and his series On the Hour *was transferred to television as* The Day Today. *In 2005 he created the political sitcom* The Thick Of It. *Other works include* The Armando Iannucci Show *for Channel 4, the HBO political satire* Veep *and the 2013 film* Alan Partridge: Alpha Papa.

I WAS VERY, VERY UNCOOL AT SCHOOL. I was more into comedy than music and bands like most of the kids. I listened to a lot of radio comedy in the late 1970s – things like *The Hitchhiker's Guide to the Galaxy* and TV stuff like *Not the Nine O' Clock News*.

I went to St Peter's Primary School in Partick, which is the school Billy Connolly went to. I remember he came back and gave a talk to the pupils when I was there. He was known in Scotland then but it was before he was really famous. I enjoyed my time at St Peter's. We lived in Byres Road in the West End of Glasgow so it was a daily walk to school. All my friends were from that area so we would hang out together. I spent a lot of time in Kelvingrove Park with my friends. We lived right next to Glasgow University and at weekends the place was dead so it was a great place to play when you were 12 years old. I remember underneath the maths department being a specially good place for hide-and-seek!

After St Peter's I went to St Aloysius secondary school in Garnethill, more in the centre of Glasgow. For about six months I had thoughts of becoming a Catholic priest. We weren't really regular churchgoers so I suppose I rebelled against my parents, as you do as a teenager. Because they were so lax, my form of rebellion was to be devout. As I say, I was the uncoolest person ever. My brothers were into football and supported Celtic but I wasn't really into sport. I rowed on the Clyde on Saturday mornings, which I always associate with the smell of beer. There was a distillery over the road and the smell was quite horrible.

I went to Glasgow University for a year then I got a place at Oxford. It was great fun at Glasgow

"One of my favourite places in Glasgow is a second-hand bookshop called Voltaire and Rousseau down a little lane off Gibson Street. There were books piled a couple of metres high – great mountains of books everywhere."

"I had my first and only taste of camping with my friends on Skye. I thought it was the most fantastic scenery I had ever seen."

University but I lived right next to it so it was just like popping down the road. It didn't feel like that big seminal moment when you leave home for the first time and you get your big taste of independence. After Oxford I came back to work at BBC Scotland HQ at Queen Margaret Drive which was great – not far from my parents. I like that whole area around the Botanic Gardens and Hillhead.

We weren't regular holiday goers when I was a kid, but every three or four years at weekends a whole bunch of Italian families – maybe five or six of us – would go off in a big cavalcade to Loch Lomond for a day trip and a picnic. I still like going up to Loch Lomond now. Once I get past St Andrews I'm not so familiar with the landscape. It's still on my list of places to explore. As a kid there would also be notorious seaside trips to Ayr and Largs. It was so damn cold, but at the time you don't think about that – you think: ice-cream and fish and chips.

By the time I was 15 or 16, being so close to Edinburgh I started going to the Edinburgh Festival. They were my first holidays with my friends and peers, I suppose. Before I discovered hotels I had my first and only taste of camping with my friends on Skye. I thought it was the most fantastic scenery I had ever seen, and then the realisation that there was no one around for miles and miles. And we were caught in one of the worst storms imaginable. We had set up our camp and pitched our tents in what looked like a patch of ground with three paths around it. It poured through the night and we discovered that those three little paths were actually riverbeds. Now they were flooding and we were marooned on a tiny island! We waded through the water and eventually found a pub and the landlord let us use his boiler-room to dry off everything. We were soaked to the skin. In the pub someone came over and told us he'd heard our story and he had a big luxury tent – it was one of those huge affairs with adjoining apartments and anterooms. His wife had just gone into labour so he had to take her to hospital and needed us to look after his tent. What a result – and it was next to a pub!

One of my favourite places in Glasgow is a second-hand bookshop called Voltaire and Rousseau with the motto: we are classy. It's the most unprepossessing place down a little lane off Gibson Street around the back of the university. There were books piled a couple of metres high – great mountains of books everywhere – but there never seemed to be any attempt to sell any. There was a warm welcoming stove and Radio 3 always playing. I bought loads of books there, which I still have to this day.

I was very proud to get my honorary Doctor of Letters from Glasgow University in 2011. All the family made a special effort to come and it was a nice surprise. It was great to be driven right past where I used to play as a kid and then to see bits of the old cloisters and other buildings that I didn't know so well and the fantastic arts collection.

I still think of Glasgow as home even though I have a family and kids of my own and we live close to London. My mum and my brothers are still in Scotland and my sister lives in London. I don't know if I'd ever move back to Scotland as my wife is English and my children always associate trips back to Scotland with atrocious weather. But they do connect with the place. My sons both support Celtic as well as following Liverpool.

If we ever did move back to Scotland it would have to be Glasgow. I like Edinburgh but Glasgow is spiritually where I belong. It's got everything you'd want. It has the culture, the people and it's accessible to beautiful countryside. I like the wit of Glaswegians. There's a great humour and cleverness with language in people like Billy Connolly, Arnold Brown, Stanley Baxter and Chic Murray. My all-time comedy hero is Woody Allen but if I had to pick a favourite Scottish comedian it would be Billy Connolly. I'm also a great admirer of Alex Salmond's wiliness and Alex Ferguson, because of his consummate professionalism.

@aiannucci

"Glasgow is spiritually where I belong. It's got everything you'd want. It has the culture, the people and it's accessible to beautiful countryside."
Glasgow University Tower

95

JIM KERR

singer

Jim Kerr – lead singer with Simple Minds – continues to record and tour with the band he set up with childhood pal guitarist Charlie Burchill in 1977. Simple Minds hit the big time with Don't You (Forget About Me) *which topped the American charts in 1985. They have notched five UK number one albums in a career spanning four decades and released* Big Music *in 2014.*

WHERE I WAS BROUGHT UP in Glasgow's Toryglen, you felt you had a fundamental duty to help, whatever it was. My grandad had been around the world with the Army, and I remember he came back saying: "I loved Cape Town; you have to see this place. But it's a shame for the poor blacks - they're not even allowed to walk on the same side of the street as you." You're only a wee boy, but some of that comes through, I think.

So I always single out the Nelson Mandela tribute concerts as a career highlight. It was probably us at our best. Another was our first gig at Satellite City in Glasgow in 1977. We played songs such as *Chelsea Girl* and *Pleasantly Disturbed*. Even then, guitarist Charlie Burchill and myself knew we were going places. Hitting No.1 in America with *Don't You (Forget About Me)* was great, too. Very few bands from our neck of the woods achieved that.

My happy childhood memories of Glasgow centre on school friends and the interaction with the rest of the kids who played together in the street. Me and Charlie met when we were eight.

> ❝ Charlie and I enjoyed every minute of our upbring in Glasgow – it's a rock and roll city

There was a guy in our class at Holyrood Secondary called Kenny Campbell and his brother was the head of security at the famous Green's Playhouse venue, even

The Clyde Arc 'Squinty' Bridge

before the Apollo. He would say to us: "Come up at nine o'clock, I'll leave the back door open."

So because we could get in free, we'd go and see anything and everything. People we didn't know like Todd Rundgren or this unknown band supporting Mott The Hoople called Queen. We'd say: "There's something about this lot, they're getting to the back of the audience. Support bands shouldn't go down a storm." From an early age, we were watching this crowd interaction thing and learning.

We originally formed as Johnny & The Self Abusers in 1977. It was the heyday of punk. The Clash and The Stranglers came to Glasgow and there were riots and the city fathers banned all visiting punk bands. But they didn't ban local ones so we were the only punks in town. We had six or seven fantastic gigs, then the day our one and only single *Saints and Sinners* came out we split up in true punk spirit. But if we hadn't done that maybe Charlie and me would be sitting in a pub now saying one day we'll put a band together. It was a catalyst.

"It's genuinely magic around the Trossachs, and if you don't go in August there's ususally no one around."

" We were soaked in that working-class industrial culture of Scotland

When we first started all we were thinking about was getting another gig as there were never any guarantees. Back in those days no one really went on forever. We are very fortunate to have had the career we've had. We never imagined we'd make it big, let alone still be going now.

I don't think we had any conception of what was going to happen. I mean back then, words like 'career' – they just didn't even enter into it. You just thought about your next single, or your next album, or the tour you were about to start.

Sometimes Charlie and I can be driving to a gig sitting beside each other in the back of a car and it's hard not to be sentimental. Sometimes it's felt like it's me and him against the world, even though we have very different lifestyles now.

We're Glasgow through and through and we enjoyed every minute of our upbringing in Glasgow. It's a rock and roll city, and we loved that environment. Scotland is special and unique. It's to do with the people, the culture and the landscape.

We were so drenched in Labour; because of my dad, we were soaked in that working-class industrial culture of Scotland. My parents were huge influences. Dad was a builder and Mum worked as a machinist in a heavy-duty garment factory. I think Scots in general are a fair-minded, warm-hearted lot. I think I was very much shaped by the times and place I grew up in. The values of the community still live on within me. And the song *I Belong to Glasgow* is a particular fave for obvious reasons.

Although we are a Glasgow band, when we started I lived in Edinburgh. At that point Glasgow never had the Sub Clubs, the King Tut's and all that. Edinburgh always had the gigs – Tiffany's, and places like that. It was particularly cool then.

And it's a magical location. We've been lucky enough to play in some fantastic places, but I'm very fond of Edinburgh. We go around the world playing great venues – but few have such a spectacular backdrop as Edinburgh Castle.

If someone had come to me when I was 18, an apprentice plumber, and said: "Here's the deal. It's going to be mad – but in return you get this," I'd have bitten their hand off. To complain about it would be really churlish. There are sacrifices, and you can't have it all. You can never have it all. But it's a great deal.

In my late teens I hitch-hiked down to London to see the Sex Pistols with my band. We didn't end up seeing them, but the lifts went so well that we ended up travelling around Europe – it was quite spontaneous. Until then I'd enjoyed my life in Glasgow but that was when I realised there was a bigger world out there.

My first holiday memory was when I was five and my parents took me to Bray in Ireland. We took the overnight boat to Dublin and stayed in a B&B. It was the first time I had a knickerbocker glory, which was even more exciting than going away for the first time. My parents would take us on day-trips to west coast towns like Ayr, Largs and Saltcoats. I can still remember the sunny days and family picnics on the beach.

I love all of Scotland really – the cities, towns, countryside and coast but I'm very fond of the Trossachs, where I lived for a while. It is genuinely magic around there, the landscape is amazing and if you don't go in August there's usually no one around. That's the sort of place I like going to these days.

Spending much time, as I have through the years, near the small town of Callander enabled me to familiarise myself with the glacial stillness of Loch Katrine and the eagle's view from the top of Ben Ledi.

simpleminds.com

"Spending much time near the small town of Callander enabled me to familiarise myself with the glacial stillness of Loch Katrine."
Walker on Ben A'an looking over
Loch Katrine, Stirlingshire

ROSS KING

presenter, actor, author

Ross made his debut in theatre aged five, on radio at 15 – he was Britain's youngest daytime host on Scotland's Radio Clyde – and on television at 17. He was entertainment anchor on KTLA in America, winning four news Emmys and a Golden Mic award. He has won two prestigious Sony awards. Now Los Angeles showbusiness correspondent on ITV1's Good Morning Britain and Lorraine, Ross is also a novelist.

I'M CLYDE-BUILT, like the ships made around Glasgow. I live and work in the US but I'm a Scot through to my bones. When I'm standing in the place I live in Los Angeles I can see the Hollywood sign from just about every window – but on the wall I have a huge pen-and-ink picture of old Glasgow. So I may be far from home but there is always that reminder.

I've been ridiculously lucky in my life. I've interviewed some huge names, I've had some exciting acting jobs and I've presented some great shows and events. But my proudest moment was when Danny McGrain, the Celtic captain, asked me to play in a special Scotland v England game at Wembley. He said he needed some pace up front! I was about 20 at the time and the only non-pro in the Scotland team. I even scored a goal. It was a real stand-out moment for me.

Football was always a big part of my life as a kid. We lived in Scotstoun in Glasgow until I was five, then we moved to Knightswood not far away. It was a big, open place with wide streets. Billy Connolly once said to me that when he first went to Knightswood he thought it was what America would be like. We had a council house with – what seemed at the time – the longest back garden in the world. Brilliant as an improvised football pitch. My friends would come over and we would keep kicking the ball until we dropped.

Sport runs deep in my family. Both of my parents loved sport, especially tennis and football, and my dad was a terrific player of both. I was a workmanlike footballer myself, and my plan when I grew up was to play as a semi-pro and work as a PE teacher at the same time.

Football is one of Ross's passions

My parents were absolutely behind me, and it seemed to satisfy the careers guidance people at school as well.

Music was the other big thing in my childhood. My mum played piano and my dad played a range of brass instruments. I was always up singing at weddings, so there was probably a bit of the entertainer in me from the start.

As I got a bit older – about 13 or 14 – I realised I wouldn't be able to make it as a footballer: I just wasn't good enough to be a professional. And, in any case, I was becoming more and more drawn to showbusiness. Again Mum and Dad were very supportive but they were worried that there was no way they could help me as we didn't know anyone in that field. But I talked things through with my maths teacher Roddy Hood (who had gone to school with the great Jack Bruce, as it happens) and he suggested I start with hospital radio.

Then a bit of luck came my way when I saw an advert for a Saturday job at our local radio station. I applied and I got it thanks to Paul Cooney (then Head of Sport who went on to become the MD). You got £10 and did everything – from making tea and coffee to photocopying scripts to setting up rigging at the football grounds for the outside broadcasts. I loved it and, instead of going to drama school, I decided to make a go of it. I went on to become a DJ on Radio Clyde and they were some very good times.

I was fortunate that I had such a strong family backing. My parents supported me in all my choices and I have a wonderful sister called Elaine. Even now, she and I speak on the phone very day. My childhood was idyllic, and we never seemed to want for anything, although there wasn't a lot of money about. Our house backed onto our school and I would wait until I heard the school bell then would run to get there on time. Not much of a commute! I imagined everyone had a family life like I had, but you find out later how fortunate you were to have such a great atmosphere around you. Maybe we were the most abnormal of normal families.

One thing Mum always used to say to me was: "Do your best – that's all you can do." It didn't seem like a special message when I was a kid but, by the time I was about 22, I realised what she meant. It's a Scottish – or maybe a north British – work ethic. You understand that the world doesn't owe you a living. You have to work for everything and earn your place in the world. When I'm giving talks to youngsters, my mum's words are the best piece of advice I can give them.

Another principle that I've lived by in my working life is: diversify. Don't put all of your eggs in one basket. A lot of my work is factual reporting and interviewing, but I've also co-written a novel called *Taking Hollywood* with my old pal and brilliant writer Shari Low. We publish under the name of Shari King – we got to number four on Amazon – and the sequel is called *Breaking Hollywood*.

I have done rather stranger things like playing Frank-N-Furter for the *Rocky Horror Show*'s 25th anniversary tour and other West End musicals and plays. I also hosted and performed at the London Palladium, and I could see my mum and dad in the front row of the balcony. They were always there for me – but they would bring me down to earth at the same time if I needed it. I remember hosting Sports Aid at the SECC in Glasgow and the place was packed with thousands of people. I was really buzzing when I spotted them in the crowd and could see Mum mouthing something at me. At first I thought she was giving me some praise, but in fact she was saying: "Speak slower."

Glasgow is a place where I have so many fantastic memories. It's a great city with a great motto – Let Glasgow Flourish. I love the Charles Rennie Mackintosh buildings and art deco design. I was devastated when one of his masterpieces – the Glasgow School of Art – was hit by fire in 2014. And I love all the theatres in the city, quite a lot of which I've played in the past, such as the King's, Pavilion and Mitchell theatres. As a kid I used

to love going to pantomimes especially to see my hero Jack Milroy.

Our holidays were always in Britain and often in Scotland. I have fond memories of the Isle of Skye. I also love St Andrews with all its history. It's a lovely place to go for a walk along the coast at night when it's lit up, and of course it has that famous golf course with the 18th fairway that you often see on TV. And it was thanks to golf that I once shook hands with Charlie Chaplin – for me, the biggest star I have ever met, although I was just a boy at the time. It was in Nairn where he used to go because of his love of golf when he was a young man. We spotted a big, black old Daimler in town and we were sure it was his because we'd heard he was there. Then one evening, in the twilight as I was walking with my mum, my aunt Betty and my sister we saw this man in a big black coat and a Homburg hat. It was him. We all walked over, introduced ourselves and shook his hand.

When I think of what I'll do later in life I see myself running a tea shop in Luss on the banks of Loch Lomond. The theme tune from the film *Local Hero* – Mark Knopfler's *Going Home* – is playing in the background and I have all my bits of memorabilia decorating the place. I'll be that sad person standing behind the counter, pointing at the photos on the walls and telling everyone my showbiz tales!

rossking.com

@theRossKing

"I see myself running a tea shop in Luss on the banks of Loch Lomond."
Cottages in Luss

DECLAN MICHAEL LAIRD
actor and model

After River City, *Declan went to the Stella Adler Academy of Acting in Los Angeles. He acted in* The Lost Purse *and* Lost Angels *films and played the lead in web series* Camp Abercorn. *He was the face of adverts for the 2014 FIFA World Cup and Chevrolet and is brand ambassador for Dunmore Scotland and Kennett watches. In 2015 he landed roles in Netflix Original series* The Bahamas *and feature film* The Rectory.

IT WAS FOOTBALL, FOOTBALL, FOOTBALL for me up to the age of 17. Sport was a big thing in my family – my older brother Stefan became a football coach and my dad is a sports agent so we had this shared passion for football and other sports. I don't know how my mum put up with all of it. Being a professional footballer was my goal from the beginning and I was delighted to be taken on by my local football club, Greenock Morton. But it all went wrong when I injured the cruciate ligament in my knee on my professional debut. I was devastated. I was told I would be able to play football again but that, by the time I was in my thirties, I could have a serious knee problem. I decided to call it quits.

It was a difficult position to be in because I'd lived for that moment and it seemed as if I'd been building up to a life in football. Kilmacolm where I grew up was perfect for me because directly opposite our house was a huge park with rugby and football pitches. Me and my friends would go there every single day and just run around, kicking a ball. There wasn't time for anything else. We'd be there until the street lamps came on and reckoned we had another 20 minutes after that to carry on before we had to go home. It was a great childhood.

So it was a huge thing for me at the age of 17 to have to look for something else. It wasn't as if I had anything else to fall back on. I have a really good work ethic but when I was at school I'd put all my concentration into football, not my schoolwork. I played the funny guy in class and didn't bother with my studies as much as I should have. I hadn't really anything else in mind. All my mates were filing applications for uni but that just never

appealed to me. I thought about maybe doing a degree in physiotherapy but it wasn't what I wanted to do.

Up until then I'd never even thought about acting but I was interested in television and I signed up for a course in TV production and writing, then I went for a part in *River City* – my first ever audition – and I got the role of Sean. Being on set on *River City* was a great thing for me. It was my first job in the entertainment industry.

My big break came by chance in 2011 when my dad had some work in the US. I had never been to America before so he asked me to come along with him and we'd have a week's holiday. We were walking down Hollywood Boulevard one day when we saw a sign asking for people to join workshops with an Oscar-winning producer at the Stella Adler Academy of Acting. My dad bet me $50 to give it a go, so I said OK and went in. I'd never had any formal acting training up until then and I really enjoyed it. The coach took me aside and said: "You are an actor." It made me realise this was what I really wanted to do. Then I was given a full scholarship at the studio – I was the first actor since Robert de Niro to get a full scholarship – so of course I said yes, and off I went just after my 18th birthday. My life just suddenly took this weird 180-degree turn.

Thinking about it now it was a big move to go out there on my own. Maybe I was naïve, but at the time I didn't even think about it. It's great being in Los Angeles, but I have never lost sight of who I am and where I'm from. I'm a Scot through and through! The majority of my friends in LA are from Scotland and Ireland – somehow we just found each other – and we often get together.

On the set of Camp Abercorn

We're like a clan. If we're in a bar and The Proclaimers' *500 Miles* comes on we all start singing along at the top of our voices and everyone else in the bar is staring at us as if we're from another planet.

That's one of things about Scots – we tend to look after each other. When I first came out to LA I got to know the Scottish presenter Ross King who is also out here. Within a week of me landing he asked me over for lunch, and now I go over to his place regularly. He's

"I love Ashton Lane in Glasgow. It looks like something off Harry Potter. There are all these bars and restaurants piled on top of each other and it's just magic. Some of my best memories are of being there with my mates."

fantastic and he's like a big brother to me – he's supportive but he doesn't let me get away with anything. If I start complaining about anything he'll say: "Declan – just shut up!"

Another Scot who's always been there for me is Jim Sweeney, an actor from Greenock who knew my dad. I met Jim for coffee in Greenock when I'd decided I wanted to get into acting and he gave me loads of advice. Since then he's been like my guardian angel. He used to go with me to auditions and I'd go to his house and he'd teach me techniques to use on camera. He took the time to help me and never expected anything in return. Even now he rings me every week. Now he has got a part in *Outlander* which is set in Scotland. It's a really popular show and there are billboards about it everywhere. I'm so pleased for him. And without the support of my parents and older brother Stefan I would never be where I am today.

Living away from my homeland really makes me appreciate it when I go back. I was so pleased to be given a best acting award by the Write Camera Action event in Glasgow in 2012 for my work in *The Lost Purse* – it made it more special because of being there. Glasgow is one of my favourite places, and I particularly love Ashton Lane. It's a cobbled lane and it looks like something off *Harry Potter*. There are all these bars and restaurants piled on top of each other and it's just magic. I used to go there a lot as a teenager bar-hopping and some of my best memories are of being there and having a laugh with my mates. Glasgow is a great city for culture as well as fun, and it's so full of character.

I'm also very fond of Aberdeen. It's known as the Granite City and maybe doesn't have a glamorous image but I used to love summer days on the beach there. Now I can go to Malibu, but it doesn't have those memories. Another place that means a lot to me is Arran where my dad is from. Living in a major city and always being busy, I love the idea of going back there and just relaxing in this quaint place and seeing the same ten faces every day.

Life is incredible in LA and sometimes I can't believe my luck, but being from Scotland I always keep my feet in the ground. Scots will never let you get above yourself. Whatever you do – whether you're in construction or you're a movie star – they treat you the same. They won't take any nonsense. If you've got your head in the clouds they'll bring you straight down to earth. My parents have always supported and encouraged me but they're the same in that respect. My mum used to call me an eejit. I've never had a tattoo, but if I did I'd have those letters tattooed on my toes so every time I'd look down I'd be grounded again.

@declanmlaird

"Arran where my dad is from means a lot to me. Living in a major city and always being busy, I love the idea of going back there and just relaxing in this quaint place and seeing the same ten faces every day."

DENIS LAW
footballer

One of Scotland's greatest-ever footballers, Denis Law loved but left his Aberdeen birthplace to carve out a magnificent career with Huddersfield Town, Manchester City, Torino and Manchester United, three times commanding record transfer fees and sharing a Scotland goal-scoring record of 30 goals in 55 games.

MY FATHER WAS A FISHERMAN who worked out of Aberdeen Harbour and as a young lad in the 1940s and early 1950s I was fascinated by the boats and the life he and his colleagues led.

To this day I have never lost that feeling for the harbour and the boats – even though, nowadays, the fishing has been replaced by the oil industry and many of the harbour areas I knew as a youngster are now cordoned off for security.

We lived in a tenement in the Woodside district of Aberdeen and it was a tough life but we were very close as a family – I was the youngest of seven, with three sisters and three brothers. We had it tough but didn't know any different and just did the best we could.

My dad George had been in the Army in the First World War and the Royal Navy in the Second World War and it had been a tough life for my mum Robina as well.

Although my first five years of life were the last five years of the Second World War, I was too young to remember the effect it had on the city.

Aberdeen was a target, with all the shipping going to Norway and so on, and the city got bombed. My one big memory of the war as a wee boy was being taken into an air-raid shelter, and wondering what was going on.

With Dad working on a trawler I would always be down at the harbour having a look round. Then one day when it was calm we sailed a few miles out – and that's when I decided it was NOT the life for me!

The boat had bunk beds in a wee circle with a wee table and up to six guys squeezed into it, and it was far from comfortable. But those were the days when fishing

Denis in action in his footballing heyday

"My love for Aberdeen and the harbour has never left me. Whenever we go back to visit we drive round the place – to me it hasn't changed."

Statue of Denis, centre, with fellow Manchester United legends George Best and Bobby Charlton

was fishing – now they have all the technology and it's more efficient, sure, but not the same as back then.

My love for the city and its harbour has never left me, and whenever we go back to visit, my wife Diana and I always take a drive round the place, and the city, seeing all the old granite buildings which are still there – to me it hasn't changed.

My last surviving sister, Frances, and my brother Joe still live in Aberdeen and we love to go back and visit them from where we live now, in Cheshire.

One of our favourite drives is the 15 miles down the coast to Stonehaven to see the harbour and castle there and down to the River Dee at Banchory.

It's a very beautiful part of Scotland and never fails to bring back happy memories. And then, of course, there's the Ashvale Chippy – you get the world's greatest fish and chips there!

I've lived in England for such a long time, and there are parts of Scotland I have always wanted to see, but never have – yet.

One of those is the Outer Hebrides, which has always been an ambition, and one which I must fulfil before I pass away. I've been as far as the Isle of Skye, but never beyond, even though there's a direct ferry to the Hebrides from Aberdeen these days.

I went away to England to play football when I was just 15 but I never got over my homesickness for a very long time. In fact, Huddersfield Town, where I first played in England, even brought an old school friend, Gordon Low, down too to share my digs and help me settle better.

As a kid, I never possessed a pair of football boots until I was nine – and then it was our next-door neighbour's son's second-hand pair that I got. But how glad I was to have those boots.

I attended Hilton School until I was ten and then Kittybrewster Primary School, and did fairly well. I won a place at Aberdeen Grammar, but football was my life by then and I turned the grammar school down because they only played cricket and rugby there. I couldn't possibly go to a school where they didn't have a football team, could I?

I went to Powis Junior Secondary instead, where they did play. My life by that time was based on football and as well as the Academy team, on Saturday I would play for the school in the morning and the Colts in the afternoon.

The thought of being a professional footballer had still never occurred to me but Archie Beattie from Huddersfield Town picked up on me in the mid-1950s and asked me to join them – I didn't even know where Huddersfield was! It was a difficult decision which my family left to me but Archie made it very clear that I would be looked after and that everything would be fine.

I didn't know what I was going to, but I decided to go, and I remember the day I left home, getting the train from Aberdeen and changing at Newcastle and York to get to Huddersfield.

I earned £5 a week and my digs were £2 2s 6d but all of a sudden we were getting breakfast each morning, which was wonderful. I returned home at every opportunity – and regularly took my washing back in a parcel for my mum to do.

As I said, I can't tell you how homesick I was – it was something I didn't get over for many years. But my football career progressed well and bit by bit I got used to it, without ever losing my love for Aberdeen and home.

I think I can safely say I enjoyed a good football career, but if anyone asks me what was my best achievement, it was that I was selected to play for Scotland.

In all the years, I always had that special, strong feeling for Scotland. Being chosen to play for, and fight for, my country at 18 – just three years after I left school – remains one of my happiest memories. That was something you could just never have expected, and Sir Matt Busby – he wasn't a Sir then, of course – was my manager, just after the Munich crash.

Today, I've been privileged to be able to put something back into the community where I grew up, and to help the young kids there.

I have put my name to the Soccer Tournament at Aberdeen Sports Village, and the Denis Law Legacy Trust for Streetsport. It's lovely to see the kids up there and hopefully some of them will be putting on the professional shirt of Aberdeen FC or whatever in the future.

It's special to be able to put your name to things like that: it's giving something back to the area where you grew up, and I've also enjoyed taking in a couple of Aberdeen games again recently at Pittodrie.

Why, I was even given an honorary doctorate from the University of Aberdeen in 2005 – it was really nice to get something like that and an unexpected honour. That's a bit special for a local lad like me.

And I was privileged, too, to take over as Patron of Football Aid from Sir Bobby Robson when Sir Bobby died in 2010. He was a wonderful fella, and I was honoured to be able to carry on his work.

Today, I look back at the old days and understand how, for all the tough life, it was good for you really. Having had that sort of upbringing, you could put up with quite a lot and I'm certain it stood me in good stead for the life and career I've had since.

"One of our favourite drives is the 15 miles down the coast to Stonehaven to see the harbour and castle there."
Dunnottar Castle

SUE LAWRENCE
writer and *Masterchef* winner

A trained journalist and avid cook, Sue combined her two passions after winning BBC's Masterchef in 1991, writing a host of cookery books, many exploring the cuisine of her native Scotland. She is a prolific newspaper and magazine columnist and has made many TV appearances, both in the UK and overseas. Her first novel is Fields of Blue Flax.

WE HAVE SOME OF THE BEST FOOD in the world in Scotland – and we're finally realising it. Ingredients like our beef, lamb, berries, oats and barley are second to none. At last the tide is turning away from the processed food I remember from my childhood when Vesta curries were the order of the day.

> ❝ We have great food in Scotland, but the worst thing I've ever eaten is guga – a Scottish delicacy

When I was researching my book *A Cook's Tour of Scotland* I tootled around the country talking to our great food producers, farmers and fishermen and seeing some of the wonderful produce we have here. You don't have to do anything fancy with it: kale, mince and tatties, black pudding, herrings, and risotto made with barley can be simply done and are all great local foods. And now there's the revival in baking and we're taking a pride in it.

I have to admit, though, that the worst thing I've ever eaten was a Scottish so-called delicacy. It was guga – baby gannet – which, in an old tradition in the Western Isles, can be hunted for a period of ten days. The traditional way to cook them is to boil them, eat them with tatties and drink cold milk with it. It was the most revolting taste. A group of friends joined me to try it and

"There is a feel of a different age about places like Lewis." Callanish Standing Stones in Lewis

The Pass of the Cattle – the highest road in Scotland

we only got through it by guzzling red wine.

It's a reminder of how people used to live on those islands and there is still a feel of a different age about places like Lewis and Harris – a charm and a gentler pace of life that is quite beguiling. I remember going there one May holiday when my three kids were little. It was wonderful weather, almost a heatwave, and we went for a stroll on Luskentyre beach in Harris. There was this white, white stretch of beach with not a soul on it except us and a few cows which just happened to be wandering there at the same time.

Shetland is another favourite place of mine, and Eshaness is particularly spectacular. Back on the west coast I love the area around Ullapool. I remember my fa-

ther used to cycle on the Pass of the Cattle at Applecross. It's one of the highest mountain passes in Scotland and you can look over towards Skye. It's a really special place.

Then there are some lovely spots near Dundee (where I was born and later went to university) like Glen Clova – JM Barrie was from around there – and Loch Brandy. I still have family in Dundee and one of the best views I know is from a relative's house overlooking the Tay and over to Fife, with fields basking in sunshine. People from outside Scotland think it rains all the time here, but we know better.

My husband used to be in the RAF and we lived overseas for many years, but when he left the service we moved back to Scotland to live in Edinburgh. The view

of Cramond Island and the city itself from the aeroplane as you sweep in tells you you're home.

But it's not just the places in Scotland that make it special – it's the people. There's an integrity about them – something I hope I learned from my father and my uncle – that I think is inspirational. No matter who you are, they will treat you the same. Underneath it all we believe, as Robert Burns wrote, that 'a man's a man for a' that'.

@suehlawrence

DENIS LAWSON

actor

Denis Lawson is best known for his roles as Gordon Urquhart in the 1983 film Local Hero, *John Jarndyce in the BBC's adaptation of* Bleak House, *Tom Campbell-Gore in BBC TV's* Holby City *and Wedge Antilles in the original* Star Wars *trilogy. In 2012 he replaced James Bolam in BBC One's* New Tricks.

I WAS JUST FIVE OR SIX YEARS OLD when I started wanting to perform. As a schoolboy my ambition was to be a song-and-dance man, an entertainer.

I don't have particularly happy memories of Crieff Primary School. Our headmaster used to come to school in a morning suit and there was a lot of corporal punishment. It was the cane or the belt if you were late for school or caught talking in the corridor.

But the head did teach us to sing in choirs and we would compete every year in Perth. I sang all the time and we would put on little plays in class. When I was 11 I played the lead in a musical version of Robin Hood. I remember standing with my parents and the head saying to them: "Denis should go into drama." That was quite remarkable for that time, really.

In a little town like Crieff we had two cinemas and I was always at the pictures. I would love watching performers on screen like Danny Kaye, Jerry Lewis, Gene Kelly and Donald O'Connor – they were my inspiration. The cinema was the only place to go. This was in the late 1950s, before television came along, so it was the radio or the movies. The pictures is what you did on a Saturday afternoon.

Sadly they were pulled down long ago but I've recently got involved with a project to bring a new cinema to Crieff. Some local guys have taken over an old library and want to turn it into a cinema and music venue and run art classes too. It's a fantastic project. I did a film workshop in the summer of 2013 there for both local schools. When I was at school there was a big social divide. It's a lot better now but I insisted that pupils from both schools acted together. That was very important to me.

The other big influence in the early days was going to Glasgow with my parents and being taken to variety shows and seeing comedians like Denny Willis.

I was born in Glasgow and my parents had very tough upbringings there during the Depression. When we went back to visit my grandparents in Glasgow I remember my sister and I used to sleep in the front room. There were still cobbles on the street and I remember the sound of the cars going over the cobbles and the headlights shining on the ceiling in the room. It seemed really exciting and romantic to me. The visits to Glasgow and my gran's front room at night imbued me with a love of cities.

My dad was a watchmaker and jeweller and he wanted to have a better life for us so we moved to Crieff, where my mother's mother lived, when I was just three.

The cast of Local Hero – *Denis is bottom row*

"There's also a beautiful walk – Lady Mary's Walk by the River Earn"

117

Denis with nephew Ewan McGregor

Crieff was a beautiful place to grow up. In those days it still had a cattle market. So it was a buzzy little town but surrounded by the most gorgeous countryside. I still love going back there now. Although I'm an urban person and have lived in London most of my life I really miss the landscape around Crieff. It's built on a hill – the Knock – and when you climb to the top you can see up to 20 miles in all directions and the views are just stunning. There's also a beautiful walk – Lady Mary's Walk by the River Earn. I'm very attached emotionally to those places. We were right on the edge of the Trossachs and close to Loch Earn.

❝ Visits to Glasgow and my gran's front room imbued me with a love of cities

Summer holidays would be spent in seaside towns like Prestwick and Greenock. We didn't go on a foreign holiday until I was about 13 or 14. We went to Spain and my father drove his little Triumph Herald all the way there – it took us about three days. But my fondest memories are definitely of the landscape around Crieff where I used to play with the other kids. Although I live in London I still feel Scotland is home.

My sister lives in Crieff so when I go back it's great to catch up with family and friends. I'm still in contact with my pals from school which, after all these years, is great. They couldn't care less about what I have achieved as an actor. We all got each other through school with a shared sense of humour. We are all very supportive of one another.

After primary school me and my sister Carol both went to Morrison's Academy which was a bit of a shame because we did no drama and the music department was abysmal. I was incredibly bored there. We were taught by a series of very dull men – they even managed to ruin Shakespeare for me.

The upside was I made great friends like Terry Rollo, who has sadly died. But other close friends who I still see to this day are Steve McColl, Pete Wallace and Colin Clark. And I did learn to play in the pipe band. If Morrison's was very ordinary, going to the Royal Scottish Academy of Music and Drama in Glasgow was extraordinary. To want to do drama so badly, then to be allowed to do it every day was incredible. I'd never been very academic or athletic at school but there I discovered that I was actually a good fencer and that I had a great facility for mime and movement. It was a revelation for me.

If my nephew Ewan McGregor got his acting gene from me, I have no idea where I got mine. Although my

Crieff

mother's father was from Newcastle and he was quite musical, I remember. He grew up in Union Street opposite a music hall and must have spent a lot of time there because he was full of Victorian poems and songs. Give him a couple of sherries and he would be up there for hours entertaining.

Ewan and I have great relationship. It was great to direct him in *Little Malcolm and his Struggle Against the Eunuchs*. I always had a feeling he was a special talent. I went to see him at the end of his second year at drama college. He was playing Orlando in *As You Like It* and I saw it with his mum and dad.

He was head and shoulders above everybody else. It was 'hairs on the back of your neck' stuff. I didn't say anything to his mum and dad because you don't want to raise hopes. But he had buckets of charisma even then and he's simply a great acting machine. So his success hasn't been unexpected – the only thing that surprised me was how fast it happened since he got his big break in *Trainspotting*. It's not easy to deal with that kind of pressure. But not only is he a brilliant actor, he is a very grounded guy.

"I really miss the landscape around Crieff. I'm very attached emotionally to those places. We were right on the edge of the Trossachs and close to Loch Earn."

PHYLLIS LOGAN
actress

Phyllis joined the Dundee Repertory Theatre after graduating from the Royal Scottish Academy of Music and Drama and went on to work in many television series, winning several awards. She has also appeared in films and was the voice of the Loch Ness Monster in the cartoon film Freddie as F.R.O.7. *She played Mrs Hughes in the six series of the hugely popular* Downton Abbey *from 2010-2015.*

I WAS BORN in Barshaw Hospital, Paisley and brought up in Johnstone just a few miles down the road. When I was three we moved to a house in a newly-built 'scheme'. As we had lived in a small two-bedroom flat up until then, it felt like we had taken residence in a mansion: three bedrooms, proper bathroom, big kitchen and two gardens – one at the back of the house and one at the front. This was to be our home until we children all left the nest, and indeed for the rest of my mother's life.

There was a large wood at the end of our street – although it seemed more like a forest when I was a child – and myself, my sister, brother and all the local children would spend long days there, playing hide and seek, making tree swings with ropes, fashioning sticks for sword-fighting and generally having a whale of a time.

We often had family gatherings at my granny and grandpa's house when I was a child, usually at Hogmanay. My uncle Robert had a beautiful tenor voice and he always sang that haunting air *Oh Rowan Tree* as we all sat rapt. Its lyrics speak to one's deeps and recall all the aspects of growing up in Scotland.

Our family holidays were mostly local as this was before cheap flights to Europe. Saltcoats was one of our destinations, on the Ayrshire coast. It seemed very exotic at the time to be able to play on the beach and splash around in the vast sea, regardless of the weather. On that occasion we had booked a self-catering apartment, so had to take everything but the kitchen sink with us! We must have looked as if we were emigrating. Day trips were always a staple of our school holidays and Largs, Millport as well as Butlin's in Ayr would also be on the agenda.

Phyllis as Mrs Hughes in Downton Abbey

"Our family holidays were mostly local as this was before cheap flights to Europe. Saltcoats was one of our destinations, on the Ayrshire coast. It seemed very exotic at the time to be able to play on the beach and splash around in the vast sea, regardless of the weather."

Millport, which Phyllis used to visit as a child

for drama school. When I was accepted, I realised this was the career I wanted to embark upon.

Being Scottish I don't do personal pride too well, but on reflection I did feel a sense of achievement when I was awarded the James Bridie Gold Medal on graduating from The Royal Scottish Academy of Music and Drama, as it was then. My only regret was that my father, who died the year before, wasn't there to celebrate my coming out as a full-blown actor.

Having lived away from Scotland for 30-plus years, I can't foresee a time when I would move back as my family life and home is in London, but Edinburgh would certainly have to be a place for consideration.

To me, Scotland has managed to maintain its own identity, whilst having a cosmopolitan feel and outlook. Being brought up in Scotland, with all Scottish influences around me instilled, I think, basic, decent values of fairness, loyalty and, of course, humour. I would say that the people of Scotland are fiercely proud of their heritage and proud to sing its praises.

I'm sure Robert Burns features in most Scots' influences and I am no exception. I remember as a child in primary school winning the Burns poetry-reading prize (as did my brother and sister before me) for reciting *To a Mouse*, a poem which I feel contains much of the Scots character and spirit. Perhaps that early success set me on my current path?

Sean Connery has to be an inspiration for any aspiring actor, particularly if Scottish. His humble beginnings were no barrier to him establishing himself as a major actor of his generation, a colossus of the film world. I have great respect and admiration for Annie Lennox. Her voice is truly a gift from the gods. The amount of plaudits and awards she has garnered is staggering, but equal to that is her tireless, passionate work and commitment to us all living in a fairer, better world.

I used to love watching the ferries and boats in Largs coming over from Millport and feeling a great sense of excitement as we were about to board with scores of other excitable children and day-trippers. Another favourite view is when driving along the shores of Loch Fyne in the early morning sunshine – it is pretty spectacular.

I hadn't thought of acting as a career until I was nearing school-leaving age. I had always been involved in the school drama club and choir and took advantage of any trips to the theatre and joined the film club too, but it had never occurred to me that I could choose acting as a profession, until a friend suggested I audition

"Another favourite view is when driving along the shores of Loch Fyne in the early morning sunshine – it is pretty spectacular."
Strachur on the east side of Loch Fyne

123

SIR MALCOLM MACGREGOR

Chief of Clan MacGregor

Malcolm MacGregor was an officer in the Scots Guards for 17 years before becoming a photographer and clan chief. Military life and photography have taken him to many places around the world. Alaska, Afghanistan, Oman, Africa and Asia have all featured in his work in addition to Scotland. Latterly he has travelled overseas representing Scotland and his clan at numerous Scottish events. He is Chairman of the Scots Guards Association and Convenor of the Council of Scottish Chiefs.

THE SCOTTISH LANDSCAPE was undoubtedly a huge influence on my decision to be a photographer. I had a small Olympus camera from a young age and would take photographs wherever I happened to be. The scenery in Scotland couldn't fail to inspire. As a family we lived in different parts of the world when my father was in the Scots Guards – Malaysia, Greece and America – but Scotland was always home and it's where I live now.

As a child those other places seemed very exotic to me, but there is no comparison between living in Malaysia, for example, and Scotland, where I spent about a third of my childhood. That's where I had a strong yearning to be and where I had a real affinity with my surroundings. We lived near Lochearnhead with Glen Kendrum as the backdrop. Everything was very outdoor-orientated. I'd spend my time clambering up hills in all seasons, going for long walks in woods, fishing and shooting. It was all very hardy and hearty.

Of course Clan Gregor and its history was always an abiding feature in our lives. Clans are something many Scots identify with very closely, especially in rural areas. There is also a strong identification with clans in places like Glasgow where many Highlanders went when employment became scarce in the old clan lands.

Clan business takes up a lot of my time. But it's a duty and a privilege to carry out whatever goes with being the MacGregor clan chief – if the cap fits, wear it! Being Chieftain of the Children of the Mist, as the MacGregors were known, is regarded as one of the most romantic titles in Scotland.

The River Findhorn in the north-east is one of the longest rivers in Scotland

"One of my favourite places is Torridon in the north-west of Scotland. I love the long treks, often in darkness, into the heart of the mountains and the strong sense of wildness that is evoked."

Nowadays there is a huge appetite from overseas for anything that's clan-related: people with Scottish ancestry in America, Canada, Australia, New Zealand and South Africa can't get enough of the history and events linked to the clans. I am the MacGregor contact here in Scotland. Highland Games held in America and Canada are far bigger occasions than in Scotland itself, with more razzmatazz. Around 20,000 people a day go to the big ones, whereas about 7,000 go to the games in

> **Being Chieftain of the Children of the Mist, as the MacGregors were known, is regarded as one of the most romantic titles in Scotland**

Braemar, which is the biggest in Scotland. At Grandfather Mountain Highland Games in North Carolina people from every clan descend and it's a huge celebration of ancestry. In Scotland clans are much more of a regional thing.

The difference between the regions and their special geography is one of the elements I love about Scotland and what makes the country so wonderful to photograph. There are so many outstanding places. When I was a child my family would nearly always take island-based holidays and I grew to love places like Mull and Skye. Runrig's *Nightfall on Marsco* – about one of the most spectacular Red Hills on Skye – is one of my favourite songs.

If you want to be a successful landscape photographer you have to have an affinity with the outdoors and a deep understanding of it, just as you would need a good appreciation of architecture and interior design if you are a photographer of houses. The different characteristics of the landscape in Scotland make the country so special. It has a vast expanse of mountains, hills and glens and also a wild coastline with rivers that go on forever. Then there are the softer areas of the lowlands. There are serious mountain ranges around Glencoe that contrast with the deep gorges of the River Findhorn. Then there are mountains that stand alone like Ben Vorlich overlooking the country around Lochearnhead where we used to live.

If you get up in the morning and look out of the window at a nearby mountain swathed in light it has a profound effect on you, and people have written about that effect. When I write it's about photography, but I'm very inspired by writers of Scottish extraction such as John Muir and Norman Maclean, who both lived in America. John Muir was originally from Dunbar and became a friend of President Teddy Roosevelt. He was one of the early conservationists and was behind the concept of National Parks in America. Norman Maclean, the son of a Presbyterian Minister from Mull, wrote the wonderful novella *A River Runs Through It*, inspired as he was to write about the Montana landscape, in connection with the untimely death of his brother, Paul.

I have also been inspired by the landscape around me, but in my case to photograph those fleeting moments. One of my favourite places is Torridon in the north-west of Scotland. I don't have any personal connections there but it's so dramatic and big. I love the long treks, often in darkness, into the heart of the mountains and the strong sense of wildness that is evoked. I also adore the Outer Hebrides, particularly Harris where the snow-capped mountains just drop into the sea. The light is the dominant spirit of the Outer Hebrides; its fresh translucence can rest in the mind for days.

malcolmmacgregor.com

"The light is the dominant spirit of the Outer Hebrides; its fresh translucence can rest in the mind for days."

DONALD JOHN MACKAY MBE

Harris Tweed master weaver

Donald John Mackay, known to all as DonJohn, has produced hand-woven Harris Tweed for over 40 years and is one of the leading exponents of the trade. He was awarded the MBE for services to the Harris Tweed industry in 2012, and the Worshipful Company of Weavers Silver Medal in 2013.

AS A BOY on the Island of Harris, I grew up learning the weaver's art from my father, who had been in the trade for many years. But even though I was pedalling under my dad's supervision at 12, and could work the loom by 14, I didn't know then that it would turn out to be my life and career.

I was always fascinated by the history and tradition of Harris Tweed and had a passion for the industry, perhaps more than I realised at that time.

We lived at Leverburgh, my birthplace. We were six brothers and two sisters, quite poor, and I used to travel up the west coast of Harris to Luskentyre to help my aunt – my father's sister – and uncle on their croft, where they kept sheep and cattle.

But when my aunt's husband died just before I left school, there came the time when I had to decide what I was going to do with my life: I decided I wanted to be a part of the industry that I loved. I was fascinated by the history of it, the community involvement – Harris Tweed is a way of life, far bigger than any one person, and a unique quality product.

After my aunt's death in 1983 I took on the property at Luskentyre, built a weaving shed, and then with my wife Maureen – we married in 1991 – we set up our own business, the Luskentyre Harris Tweed Company. That meant that, unlike my father, who did commission work for others, we were working for ourselves.

We knew that this was going to be us for evermore. We have never wanted to do anything else, and we are fortunate that we live and work in one of the most beautiful places in the world.

"The Island of Lewis might as well have been another continent for we kids who hardly ever left Harris. Now I travel up to Lewis on business a couple of times a week on average." Stornoway harbour, Lewis

"At Leverburgh we had the harbour but not the beaches, and as kids we were always warned for safety's sake not to go too near the water. But the island was a wonderful place to grow up, with so much beauty and community spirit."

129

Luskentyre is a tiny place, just a handful of houses, but it has a marvellous beach and wonderful scenery which has proved an inspiration in itself. I can go out and look at the colours and be inspired to come back and design a new tweed according to the colours I have seen. From that inspiration I have produced tweed in the colours of the heather, the green grass, and the machair lands.

At Leverburgh we had the harbour but not the beaches, and as kids we were always warned for safety's sake not to go too near the water. But the island was a wonderful place to grow up, with so much beauty and community spirit. Now, I couldn't ever imagine doing anything else. And while the industry has had difficult times, and was at a low ebb in the 1980s and again several years ago, it is now steadily becoming more and more healthy.

Today, there are approaching 200 weavers on the islands, but as recently as about ten years ago there were just 80. And the great thing is that the younger generation is taking an interest and getting involved now.

At the end of the last century there were many problems facing us, but then, in the first days of 2000, a Japanese contingent visited and placed an order for 250 metres, which they then doubled to 500. Three years later the sportswear firm Nike asked for samples and then emailed to order 950 metres. But a second email told us that was a mistake – for they actually wanted 9,500 metres and that had to be within a few days!

We needed help. And we got it from Derrick Murray at Shawbost Mill on Lewis, who, being the man he is, said it was my order to keep and he would supply the material at fair cost. By the end, that order became 20,000 metres.

When, around eight years ago, there was outside competition, Brian Wilson, the former MP, and a few locals got together very discreetly and managed to revive things. Today, production is at its highest level for almost two decades.

Now we are fortunate to be working in a thriving industry and while I received the MBE in 2012 for services to the Harris Tweed industry – an honour, though a surprise – it always grieves me that my wife Maureen, who works tirelessly alongside me, never gets any recognition.

In the old days, the Island of Lewis might as well have been another continent for we kids who hardly ever left Harris. Now, I travel up to Lewis on business a couple of times a week on average.

But when I've been away and come back into sight of Luskentyre beach and the view across to Taransay Sound – yes, without a doubt, that is the view I love best.

"When I've been away and come back into sight of Luskentyre beach and the view across to Taransay Sound – yes, without a doubt, that is the view I love best."

HUGH MACLEOD OF MACLEOD
Chief of Clan MacLeod

Hugh is the 30th Chief of Clan MacLeod, having inherited the title following the death of his father John in 2007. A freelance media director, he combines his career with management of the 42,000-acre Skye estate.

OUR FAMILY MOTTO is Hold Fast, and I am just a link in an unbroken chain of clan history that stretches back 800 years. Dunvegan is the oldest continuously-inhabited castle in Scotland and my job, with the help of my fantastic estate team, is to conserve, develop and share the MacLeod Estate legacy to the best of my ability.

Part of the sentimental value I attach to Dunvegan, albeit with far less time to indulge these days, are the many happy childhood memories of getting soaked on long walks up mountains and glens. It was a magical 'Mary Poppins' type of place for a child and we used to spend most of our school holidays here. I recall scrambling with my sister around the old overgrown Walled Garden in the rain, gorging on gooseberries, then walking down the bridle path to see my gran in The Cottage – a large, spooky house in the woods with those old diamond-shaped windows reminiscent of the Brothers Grimm.

There was one time when my sister and I camped on a rocky outcrop at the foot of the castle. We were woken by the sound of the sea lapping around our tent. We survived but the tent wasn't so lucky.

That's one of the aspects I love about this unique place: the elemental power of nature. It helps put life into perspective because it acts as a constant reminder of how transient we are. There is a seductive sense of permanence in how the castle was constructed to withstand not only Viking raids and bloody clan battles but also the fierce, gale-force winds and horizontal rain we experience during the Skye winters.

Dunvegan Castle and the Isle of Skye is my favourite place in Scotland, though the Outer Hebrides and St Kilda – due to their awesome natural beauty and the close historical connections my family has with those places – attract me greatly. Sir Reginald MacLeod, my great-great grandfather, only sold St Kilda in 1931 a year after the islanders had been evacuated at their own request. In the archive here at Dunvegan, we still have the old St Kilda rent books which reveal that the islanders used to pay their annual rent to the estate factor in puffin feathers! I visited St Kilda for the first time last year, and was blown away by its majestic wild beauty.

Although born and raised in London, I spent most of my childhood holidays at Dunvegan, always being out in nature and away from the crowded city. Living right next to the Loch Dunvegan seal colony rather than a busy road was bliss, and made me appreciate how enriching a life of contrasts is. I still enjoy my regular commute between Dunvegan and London and remember travelling on the Caledonian sleeper train to Inverness and opening the blind to the wild splendour of the hills around Aviemore. But travelling up north on the sleeper was a rare treat for my penny-conscious father John – he preferred a far more economical mode of transport; driving us up in one epic 12-hour voyage was not such fun.

In my view, the Fairy Flag is perhaps the most important relic in the castle collection. Probably from Syria or Rhodes, legend has it that this sacred clan banner has miraculous powers and, when unfurled in battle, the clan would invariably snatch victory from the jaws of defeat.

Before Sir Reginald had the Fairy Flag mounted in its sealed frame, it had spent centuries locked in a wooden casket and had become so worn due to its age that it could pass through his daughter's (later Dame Flora) wedding ring. Once, my family listened while an expert from the Victoria and Albert Museum set out his theory about its origins, including the historical evidence that the Norseman Harald Hardrada, one of the early ancestors of the Chiefs of MacLeod, had brought a famous banner back to Britain where he was killed in 1066. Reginald listened politely and then said: "Mr Wace, you may believe that, but I know that it was given to my ancestors by the fairies", to which Mr Wace replied: "Sir Reginald, I bow to your superior knowledge".

Another of the castle's great treasures is the Dunvegan Cup, a unique 'mazer' or drinking vessel dating back to the Middle Ages, which was gifted by the O'Neills of Ulster to one of the clan's most celebrated chiefs, Sir Rory Mor, for his support of their cause against the marauding forces of Queen Elizabeth I of England in 1596. Tradition has it that when MacLeod heirs come of age, they are expected to drink, in one draught without setting down or taking breath, 1.5 litres of claret from another heirloom, Rory Mor's Horn, a hollowed ox horn that has been at the castle since the 16th century. My father practised for a few months and managed this feat in one minute 57 seconds on his 21st birthday in 1956. However, I decided against the risk of alcohol poisoning and preferred instead to embark on a more sober approach to the role.

My father was a man of great warmth, talent, charisma and charm. Although he was also a man of many contradictions and his personality didn't slot neatly into that of Clan Chief, he loved Skye and was very proud of

"Dunvegan Castle and the Isle of Skye is my favourite place in Scotland."

Hugh at Dunvegan Castle

what he had achieved at Dunvegan. When he succeeded his grandmother in 1976, the estate was teetering on the brink of financial collapse and he decided that the only way to secure the estate's future was to embrace tourism and open Dunvegan on a commercial basis. By the time he died in 2007, my father had built the MacLeod Estate into one of Scotland's premier heritage attractions, pulling in well over 100,000 visitors each year with all the associated benefits that vital visitor spend brings to other island businesses in this fragile economic area. A fantastic achievement I hope to build on.

That period was incredibly difficult for my father. Tasked with such a Herculean challenge, he certainly did not feel a phased restoration of Dunvegan was possible. Forty years ago he might have received 75 per cent of the total cost from grant aid; now it is 30 per cent

and falling. Although he felt unjustly vilified for taking tough decisions to save an iconic part of Scotland's built heritage and one of Skye's largest private sector businesses, the abortive Cuillin mountains sale alerted the world to the huge challenges that businesses like Dunvegan face. To his credit, my father did manage to 'Hold Fast' to the rock.

Despite receiving 35 per cent of total cost grant aid funding from Historic Scotland, the estate's debt levels increased as a result of the £1.4m investment in the castle and garden restoration works and other large-scale capital investment projects. Having no other funding option available, I decided to mortgage/release equity from my London property to invest in Dunvegan in order to conserve the fabric of the building which was in a very poor condition due to the failure of the roof, windows

and cement harling. The wider estate was also in a parlous state and I decided to invest all the fruits of our seasonal labours in order to reverse decades of underinvestment. Although still a work in progress, I am very proud of what we have achieved to date and Dunvegan has recovered its rightful place as a world-class heritage attraction with a four-star Visit Scotland grading.

In July 2014 it was a very special honour for my family to welcome HRH The Princess Royal to Dunvegan, 58 years after Her Majesty The Queen came to luncheon with Dame Flora, on the occasion of my father's coming of age, at the first Clan MacLeod Parliament in 1956. The Princess met clansfolk and kindly undertook the official opening of my father's Memorial Gazebo.

My Dunvegan workload has diverted around 70 per cent of my time away from my media career. Film is a very tough profession requiring bucketloads of commitment, talent, patience and luck; for that reason, I see it more as a vocation than a job and after Dunvegan, it is my main passion.

There are many branches of the Clan Society, and Dunvegan Castle continues to extend a warm Highland welcome to those people from the clan diaspora who make the pilgrimage back to their ancestral homeland. The fact that they come is largely thanks to my greatgrandmother, Dame Flora, a charismatic Chief of the Clan MacLeod and a pioneer of what Visit Scotland brand The Homecoming. She travelled all over the world to meet clansmen and women, help them reconnect to their Highland roots and encourage them to visit the home of their ancestors. They have been coming ever since and we owe her a debt of gratitude for her key role in putting the Isle of Skye on the map in the post-war years when it was largely unknown.

dunvegancastle.com

VAL MCDERMID
writer

An award-winning writer whose work spans a variety of genres, Val is best known for her crime fiction. It is seen as part of the Tartan Noir genre which includes Ian Rankin's Rebus *series. Val's Hill/Jordan series was adapted for television and named* Wire in the Blood. *She is also a regular broadcaster and sponsor of a literary festival and Raith Rovers Football Club.*

I FEEL I WAS LUCKY to have been brought up in such a beautiful country as Scotland. It's got a magnificent, mixed landscape with beaches and islands, the emptiness of the far north-west, Perthshire and the Borders with their wee secret valleys and villages.

For me, the Scottish landscape is inextricably linked to literature. It's very organic. Many of Ian Rankin's books couldn't really be set anywhere else but Edinburgh, and Norman MacCaig has such strong links to Sutherland. I love his poetry, and, inspired by it, I spent a wonderful summer in Assynt. I found work in a hotel and in my time off I spent my time climbing hills and mountains in the area and I felt a great freedom. I particularly love the Suilven mountain in Sutherland. It's spectacular.

Scotland is different – there is no doubt about that – and it's not about sentiment or tartan or a shortbread-tin view of the country. It goes deeper, into history, religion, politics. There's a lot of common ground between us. It's quite separate to life in England. I lived in England for many years but I never really felt it was my home. When I came back to live in Scotland recently and moved to Edinburgh it felt as if my shoulders dropped and I could really relax.

I was brought up in Kirkcaldy but also spent weekends in East Wemyss in Fife with my grandparents. I loved living by the sea. My grandparents' home was ten minutes' walk from the beach and there was also woodland and country walks and a huge park in the middle of town. The East Wemyss caves near where my grandparents lived feature in my book *A Darker Domain* and are among my favourite places in Scotland. It's where I grew up and there is something mysterious and strange

The caves from Castle Green with Macduff Castle above

and wonderful about them. Fife is a beautiful part of the country with the coast, the Lomond hills, St Andrews and Crail.

When I was a child we had a big dog, a labrador retriever, and I would always take him with me, the idea being that as long as you had the dog with you, you were safe. I would set off in the morning with a duffle bag and a packed lunch – on my own, except for the dog. I suppose I was quite solitary. Because I lived in two places

I had a foot in both camps but a circle in neither. I was an only child who had to spend a lot of time around adults talking about boring things so I lived in my head. I was interested in things of the imagination.

In some respects I had quite a parochial life. Fife was very self-contained. Until they built the road bridges it was a long way from anywhere. Going to Edinburgh and Dundee was quite an adventure.

We didn't really do holidays when I was growing up,

writing. I did write some poetry, but it was the kind of thing that everyone does when they are teenagers.

One of the biggest influences in my life at that time was my English teacher Wilf Allsop. My school was very sniffy about the idea of me going to Oxford, saying that people like us don't do things like that and I wouldn't get in anyway – but he really believed in me. He gave up his spare time to coach me and I did make it. He and his family are close friends and I still see his widow on a regular basis. If he hadn't got behind me I'm not sure I'd have got there.

Going to Oxford was a huge culture shock for me – the way of life was different, the climate was different and the people spoke differently. I had to moderate my accent so people would understand me. It was a real Doppler shift in my life. As the first state school student from Scotland to go to St Hilda's College I felt it was a chance to prove my worth. St Hilda's was quite an egalitarian college. I felt the keys to the kingdom were somehow there, and I was determined to get my hands on them. It was a great experience for me, and I learned things there that have been useful throughout my life.

I've had a few special moments in my life, but I think the proudest was when I was made a fellow of St Hilda's College. For me it was huge big deal, an imprimatur, that said: "You have arrived."

But I had never had a chip on my shoulder. I grew up in a house where the message was that I was as good as anybody else and if I worked hard enough, I could do what I wanted. It's a Scottish Presbyterian thing – work hard and you'll be rewarded. There is also a sense that when you have success you should put something back. A lot of Scots have strong ties to the community where they grew up. You are aware that you are standing on the shoulders of the people of that community and that's how you got to where you are. It's not because you are so brilliant and talented. You have got a hinterland and you lose it at your peril.

Music played a big part in my life in that community. My dad was a singer, a tenor in the Bowhill People's Burns Club Concert Party, and when we were driving in the car – in the days before car radios – we would both sing together, endlessly. At one time I used to play guitar and sing in folk clubs, although I don't any more.

My favourite piece of music that says 'Scotland' to me is *The Bluebell Polka* by Jimmy Shand. It's played a lot

at ceilidhs, and I love a good ceilidh. Jimmy was a friend of my grandfather's and his music was something I was conscious of when I was a child. So this piece of music has a family connection and I also love it because it's archetypically Scottish with its tongue in its cheek – it's the Scotland of Oor Wullie and The Broons.

My family was very important to me, and my dad was a particularly strong influence. He died before my first book was published when I was 32 and that's still sad for me. He was a football scout for Raith Rovers and he would take me to matches. For me, at least, Raith Rovers is bred to the bone and it's always been part of my life. People say: "If you like football so much, how come you support Raith Rovers?" – but it's a cross I bear gladly. I sponsor the home strip and the McDermid stand there is named after my dad.

■ valmcdermid.com

although we did go to Blackpool for a week and that was my first experience of 'abroad'. More often than not we'd go to caravan parks in places like Stonehaven. I remember one such trip to Pitlochry when it rained all week and I was stuck in a caravan with a cousin I didn't like very much playing Old Maid and Beggar My Neighbour.

I used to spend a lot of time in libraries and as soon as I realised that books didn't just appear by magic – someone has to create them – I could see that there was maybe a living to be made out of writing. But I didn't write anything in particular at a young age – I just made stuff up in my head. I think it happened when I started high school and learned about composition and creative

"I particularly love the Suilven mountain in Sutherland. It's spectacular."

139

JIM MCLEAN

songwriter and record producer

Jim is best known as the writer of the 1963 ballad The Massacre of Glencoe. *He worked as a record producer in the 1960s and 1970s for labels including Decca and Fontana with folk acts including The Dubliners and comedians Little and Large. He is credited with discovering The Nolans. As The Singing Nolans they recorded an EP* Silent Night *for Jim's own Nevis label in 1972 before changing their name to The Nolan Sisters in 1974.*

WATCHING THE 2015 EDINBURGH TATTOO on BBC TV I was quite surprised to hear my ballad *The Massacre of Glencoe* introduced by Bill Paterson, played by the massed pipes and drums. It's been recorded hundreds of times by many artists over the years, of course – The Corries' version is probably the best-known – but in the 1960s the BBC would have censored my lyrics as did Kenneth McKellar when he recorded it as late as 1993 on a Lismor CD, *McKellar Today*. The verse about King William of Orange was left out. Rather than treating the subject romantically, as many did, my version laments the fact that King William signed the death warrant for the massacre. It's a rebel song with a strong Republican slant.

My first memory at the age of three is collecting shrapnel on Canal Street with my brother Robert who was six. A parachute bomb had been dropped over Paisley not far from our house. His school was hit and a neighbour's son, who was an ARP warden, was killed. When Clydebank was attacked my grandfather Wallace would walk through Paisley during the raids to make sure we were OK. We were all holed up in our tenement close and the sky was red with flames.

Over the bridge from our 18s-6d-a-week (about 92p) tenement was the burial place of Robert Tannahill, the famous Paisley poet who died in 1810. I passed his weaver's cottage every day on the way to school. My father was a minor poet himself and there is a saying that if you fling a stone up in the air in Paisley it will land on a poet. He couldn't read music – he didn't know a hatchet from a crochet as we used to joke – but he bought

a piano for half-a-crown a week with his Army demob money and I used to run home from school every day to practise on it for two solid hours. I left school at 15 so I'm pretty much self-taught in terms of literature and history. I didn't go to university until I was 50 to study for an electronic engineering degree but I've no regrets. As an apprentice radio – and later TV – engineer I was making decent money and that knowledge of electronics and music served me well when I became a record producer.

We left Canal Street when I was 15 and moved up to a housing scheme on the Gleniffer Braes. The view from there is stunning. You have this wonderful panorama – you can see right over the Clyde valley and see the shoulders of Ben Lomond, situated at the head of Loch Lomond, just peering over the Old Kilpatrick Hills. Tannahill used to wander up there and wrote lots of songs featuring the Gleniffer Braes, Stanely Castle and its environs. It's a national park now but when I was a teenager it was known as a favourite courting spot. My father and brother and I had a TV aerial business and I had a van so I'd park up there and enjoy the spectacular views. It always seems to come back to Tannahill for me. I did a Scottish Ethnology master's degree at the University of Edinburgh on the melody of one of his songs, *The Braes of Balquhidder*, when I was 70.

Burns said: "The story of William Wallace poured a Scottish prejudice into my veins which will boil along until the floodgates of life shut in eternal rest." I have two volumes of books of *The Life of William Wallace*, printed in 1830, that I've carried with me since I was a kid and

they've been with me all over the world. They belonged to my grandfather who was a Wallace and I was named after him: James Alexander Wallace McLean. Reading them from an early age I've always taken a Republican line and been politically aware. I did six months in Barlinnie prison for refusing to do my national service during the Suez crisis in 1956/7. I registered as a conscientious objector, and for refusing to do your medical they do you for contempt of court. We sewed mailbags all day – eight stitches to the inch. It was pretty tough but I quite enjoyed it in a way.

Not surprisingly, after six months inside, I travelled a lot. In Europe I spent a wonderful year in the walled town of Rothenberg in Germany and even joined the Swedish Merchant Navy for a spell. But in 1961 I came back from Denmark with a Danish friend Ole and we headed for Mull, the home of my forefathers. We lived in the youth hostel in Tobermory for a week or two until we got work as labourers constructing the new pier at Craignure, about 20 miles down the east coast of Mull. We rented a caravan from a Mrs MacLean overlooking the bay of Tobermory and stayed there for a few months. We were collected in the morning by the work van and driven down the coast through Salen, which had a dance at the weekend. The whole time seems lost in a whisky daze – whisky for breakfast in our porridge, whisky at lunchtime and whisky in the MacDonald Arms in the evening. Closing time was 9pm then but quite often the landlord would "forget" to shut the door and we would be flung out later by the Tobermory polis. The views in Mull are stupendous. Overlooking Tobermory Bay from

"*The view from Gleniffer Braes is stunning. You have this wonderful panorama – you can see right over the Clyde Valley and see the shoulders of Ben Lomond situated at the head of Loch Lomond, just peering over the Old Kilpatrick Hills.*"

Glencoe

yard so the money helped keep them going. I remember talking politics with Jimmy Reid in the canteen. In those days he was a working-class British socialist but I was interested to see that before he died in 2010 he had some years before become an SNP member supporting Scottish nationalism and independence.

The figure who inspired me most was Hugh MacDiarmid. I met him around 1960 and we became great friends. His sheer intellect and his incredible use of language was so impressive. I still have lots of the letters he wrote to me over the years before he died in 1978. He wrote in what he called synthetic Scots, amalgamating different dialects and voices from all over Scotland into a strong Republican line. I remember recording him reciting his own poetry and Burns for an LP *The Legend and the Man* and he wrote the sleeve notes to my first collection of songs called *Scottish Republican Songs*.

I've still got lots of relatives in Scotland from Dornoch in the Highlands to Glasgow. I've lived in London most of adult life with my wife Alison, children and now grandchildren so it would be impossible to move back to Scotland but I'll definitely go back on the day they declare independence. There's no question it's going to happen. It's inevitable.

Oh, cruel is the snow that sweeps Glencoe
And covers the grave o' Donald
Oh, cruel was the foe that raped Glencoe
And murdered the house of MacDonald.

They came from Fort William wi' murder in mind
The Campbell had orders King William had signed
"Put all to the sword," these words underlined
"And leave none alive called MacDonald."

Extract from *The Massacre of Glencoe*
by Jim McLean 1963

the caravan was incredible, and Craignure Bay is also very beautiful, dominated by Duart Castle, which belongs to the Clan MacLean Chief.

I started writing rebel songs in 1959 – met guys like Josh MacRae and Dominic Behan – and Pete Seeger produced a load of my rebel stuff included in an LP in America called *Ding Dong Dollar*. My songs were actually getting banned in Glasgow so ironically I had to go to London in 1966 to record them. And from then I worked as a record producer for Decca and Fontana before setting up my own label Nevis with Bill Farley in 1972. Recording Little and Large, The Nolans and Kenny Ball were the money-spinners that allowed me to do folk albums, which made no money at all. I was proud to help Jimmy Reid and the Upper Clyde shipyard workers in 1972. We did a concert for them with The Dubliners in Govan and I was asked to do a fundraiser so we got a bunch of musicians together including Alex Campbell, Dominic Behan and Ian Campbell, and I wrote a couple of political songs for it. The album was called *Unity Creates Strength*. We sold them 1,000 copies for 50p each and they sold them for £1 or so each so it was a good fundraiser for their work-in. They chose to work rather than go on strike to show the viability of the

"The views in Mull are stupendous. Overlooking Tobermory Bay from the caravan was incredible, and Craignure Bay is also very beautiful, dominated by Duart Castle which belongs to the Clan MacLean Chief."
Duart Castle

143

BILLY MCNEILL MBE
footballer

In 1967 as Celtic captain Billy, nicknamed Cesar, was the first British footballer to lift the European Cup. He won nine Scottish League Championships, seven Scottish Cups, six Scottish League Cups and 29 caps for Scotland. He made 790 appearances, playing every minute and never being substituted. He managed Celtic and won the league and cup double in 1988, the club's centenary year. He was voted Celtic's greatest ever captain and is the club's first-ever ambassador.

MY FIRST MEMORY of the view over the Cumbraes from Haylie Brae was as a young player with Celtic, travelling to Seamill Hydro Hotel for the first time. The spectacular vista of the island of Great Cumbrae and the Firth of Clyde caught my attention and has stayed with me ever since. Often I stop the car when I reach the Brae and spend a few moments peacefully taking in one of the most wonderful sights I have encountered in my travels. The combination of the far Argyll shores, the multi-coloured sea and the Cumbrae islands makes a picture that is typical of Scotland. I take great pride in being Scottish and this view truly represents the beauty of our land.

I was born in 1940 in my grandparents' house in a miners' row in Bellshill just outside Glasgow. It was a great place to grow up. I remember running to the top of the coal heaps and always playing football as a boy. I had a tremendous childhood. We left Glasgow when I was about 10 or 11 because my dad was in the Army and we went to married quarters in Hereford. It was the exact opposite of Bellshill – very stylish with beautiful buildings. We lived there for two-and-a-half years then we came back to Scotland.

I went to Our Lady's High School in Motherwell. Glasgow was a fair distance so any senior games I went to see were at Motherwell's Fir Park. It was never full unless Celtic or Rangers were playing them. The first game I remember seeing was against Aberdeen and I saw Charlie Tully play. He was different class – a real star. Early visits to Parkhead would be with my Auntie Grace. I remember being in the Jungle this one time and when the crowd swayed she lost her shoe. The buses used to

park way up London Road. It was a dismal wet day and Auntie Grace, one shoe on and one shoe lost, had to walk up to the bus in the pouring rain!

In my final year at Our Lady's High I was called up for a Scotland schoolboy game. We played England and won 3-0. Jock Stein was a spectator and he put pressure on Sir Robert Kelly to sign me for Celtic in 1957. Then I was sent out to Blantyre Victoria for a season. It was hard but I really enjoyed it.

I made my competitive debut for Celtic against Clyde in the Scottish Cup. I was a part-timer – you trained on a Tuesday and Thursday. There were two lights – one on the main stand and one on the Jungle – and you just ran around the track. That was training. Then big Jock Stein revolutionised training by letting us work with the ball. In 1960 he left for Dunfermline but then he came back to manage us in 1965. By then I was captain and I just knew something exciting was going to happen. That year we beat Dunfermline, and I scored the winner, to give us the Scottish Cup – our first trophy since 1957. But it was Jock's approach to that final which was unusual for those days. We went down to Largs and spent a whole week in preparation and talked about how we were going to play and approach the game. The supporters could sense it was the start of something big when we won our first league title in a dozen years the following year.

Preparation for our greatest-ever season started with a five-week trip to America and Bermuda. Jock's method for preparing the team and bonding was superb and he developed a keen determination among the squad. He also had great belief in our ability. We could score from

Billy holds aloft the European Cup

"If there's a better football club in the world than Celtic I haven't seen it yet."

anywhere and that was down to the way he let us express ourselves. When we won the European Cup in 1967 we were very much the underdogs. Nobody expected us to go to Lisbon and beat Inter Milan in the final. We became known as the Lisbon Lions, the 11 men – all born within a 30-mile radius of Glasgow – who defeated mighty Inter 2-1.

I remember being in the tunnel before the game. The Inter team looked daunting in their immaculate jerseys and with their tanned faces. The echo in the tunnel of 22 players and the three officials' studs clattering on the stone tiles was really loud and noisy. The referee took us up towards the final few steps then stopped and held us back. It seemed to be an eternity. I'm never happy waiting in the tunnel at the best of times. I was desperate to get out onto the pitch. We needed something to relax us and wee Bertie Auld came to the rescue. He started singing the Celtic song! Then all the rest of the lads joined in. I looked at the Italian boys and they looked astounded. I think that gave us an edge before we got on the pitch.

After their early penalty went in Big Jock had a go at us at half-time and we just took the game by the scruff of the neck. It was a great victory. If I could change anything that day it would have been for the team to do a lap of honour after the game. All the lads were in the dressing room and big Jock sent me out to get the cup. So I held the cup aloft among the fans on my own! I remember all the fans helping me up the stairs. I was looking for the players' wives but couldn't see them. I held the trophy high above my head but I have no idea where I got the strength to do it. It was a wonderful moment. I could see our fans everywhere – a sea of green and white – and the Milan fans applauding us too.

If winning the European Cup was a career highpoint as a player another as a manager was winning the Scottish Championship in the club's centenary year in 1988. It was fabulous, a fairytale come true. And if there's a better football club in the world than Celtic I haven't seen it yet.

Interview courtesy of Celtic Football Club

celticfc.net

"The combination of the far Argyll shores, the multi-coloured sea and the Cumbrae islands makes a picture that is typical of Scotland."
Haylie Brae

PETER MORRISON

musician

As one of the founding members of the Peatbog Faeries in 1991, Peter has been playing pipes and whistles in the award-winning band for more than 20 years. He is also the band's main writer. The Peatbog Faeries are particularly acclaimed as a live act, performing all over the world and representing Scotland at a host of international events. Back home they are veterans of the annual Celtic Connections festival in Glasgow.

I'VE LIVED ON THE ISLE OF SKYE all my life and have always loved the place. As a musician travelling around the world, I'm often away for quite long spells. But coming back home is always something I look forward to and I appreciate Skye more and more as time goes on.

For some people it may seem a little quiet and a lot of islanders leave for the bright lights elsewhere, but just as many stay and that is part of what makes Skye so special – people really feel they belong there.

Some of my favourite places in Scotland are on the island. We've got 360 miles of coastline so there is plenty to choose from, but I find the views from Greep Hill are particularly spectacular: you can see all round the peninsula as well as the islands of Eigg and Rum in the distance. It's astonishing. Neist Point with its lighthouse and dramatic scenery is another beautiful spot. It's well known for the views and no wonder.

When I was a child there were no mobile phones, internet, Playstations or even much telly, so I spent most of my time outdoors with my friends, fishing and clambering around rocks and cliffs. The roads were different then – often just single tracks – and there was little traffic so it felt safe. I remember at Halloween we would go round every single house in Roag – probably about 40 of them – and we never felt in any danger.

Like most people from Skye I grew up surrounded by music. In the Highlands every child up to the age of eight gets a chance to learn to play the pipes so, in primary school, I began to learn. I was actually put back a year because my fingers were too small, but I kept on

View from Neist Point on Skye to the Uists in the Outer Hebrides

"Neist Point with its lighthouse and dramatic scenery is another beautiful spot. It's well known for the views and no wonder."

trying. Something spurred me on to keep playing, even when other kids were giving it up for other instruments like guitars, drums and accordions. I was always fascinated with the pipes, ever since hearing local pipers Norman MacLeod and John Laing pipe in Santa at our annual primary school Christmas party.

Playing the pipes is a lot of effort – it's physically quite hard work – but it never occurred to me to give them up. When I was a teenager there was a strong music scene in Skye centred on the wilder ceilidh type of music more than the tunes of Scottish country dance music. All around Scotland there were bands like Silly Wizard starting up who were making an impression on younger audiences. I got involved in all sorts of bands before starting the Peatbog Faeries in 1991.

❝ Coming back home is always something I look forward to

I never dreamt I would actually be able to become a professional musician, especially as a piper. The pipers I knew would always have regular jobs. In the past the best a piper could have hoped for would have been becoming a court musician for a clan chief. So it was as much about luck as talent that traditional music became my professional life as well as my hobby. I was exposed to the right people in the right place at the right age.

I've never been one to have heroes, but it's the local players who inspired and helped me musically who I'd put on a pedestal, such as Nicol Campbell. He was a musician and a larger-than-life character in Skye, with a big moustache and a kilt. When he passed away his widow gave me his kilt, which I now wear on stage, so I take a bit of him with me. To me, the local players like Ian MacDonald, Peter MacSween and Peter Mac-Caskill were much more important than those more widely known on the folk scene.

I think most Scottish people have a strong sense of identity linked to their home area. Many Scots tend to be clued up about their history, certainly in places like Skye and the rest of the Hebrides. Unlike a lot of countries in Europe where there has been a lot of change and upheaval, we have a long history and an abiding culture – despite some skirmishes along the way.

peatbogfaeries.com

Peter playing the pipes

150

"Some of my favourite places in Scotland are on Skye. We've got 360 miles of coastline so there is plenty to choose from."
The Old Man of Storr, Skye

DAVID MOYES
football player and manager

A former centre-half for Celtic, David played for several other clubs, including Dunfermline Athletic and Preston North End where he later became manager. He managed Everton for 11 years, winning the League Managers Association Manager of the Year award three times in that spell. He left in 2013 to manage Manchester United and joined Real Sociedad in Spain as manager in 2014.

FOOTBALL WAS MY WORLD AS A KID, and it still is. The journey has taken me from Partick near Glasgow to different clubs in England and now San Sebastian in Spain. If there's one thing I've learned it's that you never stop learning. It's a whole new culture here – not just the language, but the whole way of life and the footballing philosophy as well. I'm enjoying it.

In Britain we are big importers of football talent – both players and managers – from Europe and elsewhere, but we don't seem to be big exporters. There have been some great pioneers in Europe, though, including Sir Bobby Robson, Terry Venables and Steve McClaren, not forgetting my fellow Scot Jock Wallace who managed Seville. I always hoped if I was good enough to become a coach and manager I would like to prove what I could do abroad, and that's why I chose to come to Spain.

As well as Jock, Scotland has produced a lot of notable and successful managers like Bill Shankly, Sir Matt Busby, Jock Stein, Jim McLean, Craig Brown and, of course, Sir Alex Ferguson. In 2011 the English Premier League had six or seven Scottish managers. It's hard to pinpoint exactly why, but Scotland has always delivered very good quality training to coaches; Jose Mourinho did some of his badges in Scotland. But there has to be more to it than that. Maybe there's something else about us Scots: our upbringing, a certain toughness and a thirst for knowledge. Then there's a hard work ethic, communication and wanting to do the right thing.

Being a good communicator is probably the most important attribute, and you have to have a bit of front. Sir Alex, Andy Roxburgh and Craig Brown are all excellent

David in action for Dunfermline

communicators – people who want to pass on their knowledge and know how to do it. It's also something you can learn about and improve on. I remember as a youngster with Celtic I had to speak at dinners and to supporters. When you're only 15 it can be a really daunting and difficult thing to do, but you're just told to get on with it – so you do. If you can handle that you can thrive.

That 'get on with it' lesson is a good one to learn when you're young. As I said, football was my life then and that's all I really wanted to do. My mum and dad were happy for me to just get on with it. Just about every spare hour I'd be kicking a ball around in the park at the end of our road. I went to the Boys' Brigade and played for them, I played for Glasgow schools, Scotland under-18s and I was captain of Celtic Boys' youth team. I didn't really think about making a career out of it at the time – you relied on other people to notice you and make that decision for you. All I knew was that I loved the game.

"I loved Glasgow and have great memories of it: the streets, shopping with my mum, the nightclubs when I was a bit older, even the underground."

David with the press in hot pursuit

Most of the boys round where we lived in Partick felt the same so most of my early memories are of football. We'd also go to the cinema on a Saturday afternoon and watch a matinee if we weren't watching or playing football. It was a close community in those days, but the main industry on the Clyde was shipbuilding and it was on the decline. Dad and Mum always worked – in most families both parents had to work to make ends meet. Everybody had a very similar standard of living, but people were also starting to look to enhance their lives for their families. We lived in a close but people were wanting their own front and back door and a bit of garden.

So we moved to Bearsden, which was a more up-market area. My dad was a lecturer at Anniesland College in Glasgow. I used to travel on my own from Bearsden by train to Queen Street in Glasgow, then get the number 64 bus out to Parkhead twice a week. I loved Glasgow and have great memories of it: the streets, shopping with my mum, the nightclubs when I was a bit older, even the underground. We used to have school trips to Edinburgh to see the castle and the sights but we always thought we were the better city. The people who we saw as representing Glasgow were comedians like Billy Connolly and the character Rab C. Nesbitt – people you can laugh at but admire at the same time.

When I left Glasgow I was enjoying my time at Celtic but I wasn't playing regularly enough and I wanted to play, not sit in the reserve team for a lot of the time. So I chose at the age of 20 to go to Cambridge United, which was then in the Second Division – now known as the Championship. It was a good league with good teams. I enjoyed it there. I made some good friends, people I'm still in contact with. Cambridge is a lovely place, although it isn't really renowned as a great footballing city.

I was interested in every aspect of the game when I was playing, and started taking my coaching badges when I was 20 years old. I was a qualified coach by the time I was 22 and I hoped it would make me a better player. I had been captain at most of the clubs where I played, and I was a thinker about the game as well as a player. When I was at Bristol City I coached one of the local pub teams and would take them training one evening a week.

I just loved football – playing, watching, going to games. I followed the Scottish national team and was a big supporter of Scotland, especially as a boy. One of the songs that always reminds me of Scotland is *Ally's Tartan Army*, the World Cup song of 1978. Other tunes that bring back memories are the music for Scottish country dances like the Gay Gordons and the Dashing White Sergeant. Back in the day at school we learned those dances, like they used to have in old-fashioned dance halls. We were taught how the boys would stand on one side and the girls on the other and the boys had to walk over and pick a girl. Dating has changed a lot since then!

One of the places in Scotland that holds strong memories for me is Loch Lomond. I met my wife in Balloch to the south of the loch. When we're in the area we always try to pay a visit there if we get a chance.

"One of the places in Scotland that holds strong memories for me is Loch Lomond."

EVE MUIRHEAD

champion curler

After winning four junior world championships and being voted BBC Scotland's Young Sports Personality of the Year in 2009, Eve went on to win the 2011 European championship and 2013 world championship as skip of the Scotland team. She won a bronze medal in the 2014 Winter Olympics – the youngest-ever skip to win an Olympic medal.

CURLING WAS SEEN AS A BIT ODD when I was at school. Very few people played it and some people would turn up their noses when I'd go off to practise, but it never bothered me. I loved the sport then and I still love it now.

It has been part of my life for as long as I can remember. We would go and watch my dad in curling matches from a very young age. Mum used to drive me and my brothers there – even when they were screaming from the pram. My dad was an international curler and an inspiration to me. Curling was founded in Scotland so it's important to the country and that makes it particularly special. It's become huge in Canada where a lot of the top players are from. It's a very social sport and it has meant I've travelled all over the world to play and compete.

I think curling came into the spotlight a bit more in 2002 when Rhona Martin won gold at the Olympic Games. That certainly gave it a boost and it's getting bigger. People can see it's a great sport and I'd like to think I've been able to contribute a bit to its popularity.

I grew up in Blair Atholl on my family's farm. I had a very outdoor childhood and for as long as I can remember sport was part of it. I was lucky enough to play other sports to a decent standard, and golf was the main one apart from curling. I would play golf in the summer and curl in the winter and that was fine for a while. I knew from a young age that sport would be my future. I wasn't particularly academic – I'd say I was about average – but I was always the sporty one in class. As I grew older I realised I'd have to make a choice between curling and golf if I was to do either professionally. I chose curling, but I still play golf.

"I grew up on our farm in Blair Atholl. There is the famous castle, but it's the surrounding countryside and hills that I think of – the whole environment is lovely and it's great to walk around."

The two sports are both big in Scotland and there is a lot of support and interest around the Scottish curling team, although we're not really treated any differently by everyone at home. Scottish people can be quite hard and they have this attitude that means they take no nonsense from anyone!

I travel all the time so I try to make the most of my time at home in Scotland. It's a great, great country and I can't see a time when I would ever want to leave it. There are places that hold special memories for me. Obviously Blair Atholl where I grew up is one of them. There is the famous castle, but it's the surrounding countryside and hills that I think of – the whole environment is lovely and it's great to walk around. I've also got good memories of holidays in Lossiemouth. I don't know why I remember it so well, but it has a lovely beach and I think of it fondly.

Curling wasn't seen as a cool thing to do when I was at school, but playing the pipes was. Boys and girls in more or less equal numbers played pipes and it's something I've enjoyed doing and competing in for years and years. It started with one of my friends who wanted to learn the side drum and I chose the pipes. Again, it's something that has taken me round the world.

"Curling was founded in Scotland and that makes it particularly special."

"I've got good memories of holidays in Lossiemouth. I don't know why I remember it so well, but it has a lovely beach and I think of it fondly."

159

JUDY MURRAY
tennis player and coach

Judy was Scottish National Coach for tennis from 1995-2005 and was appointed captain of the British Fed Cup team in 2011. She used to coach her sons Jamie and Andy, now both Wimbledon champions. In her playing career she won 64 titles in Scotland. After competing in BBC's Strictly Come Dancing, *Judy returned to tennis and works tirelessly to promote the sport to youngsters in Scotland.*

SCOTLAND DOESN'T REALLY 'DO' TENNIS. It's seen as a minority sport here, yet we have two grand-slam – and Wimbledon – champions in Andy and Jamie. Who'd have thought it? I'm so proud of what they have both achieved as individuals, but my proudest moments are when they play doubles together in the Olympics or the Davis Cup.

It's great that they've brought attention to the sport and that people are enjoying their success, but they won't be on the circuit forever. I think it's incredibly important that we keep on looking for champions of the future in Scotland. There's nothing wrong with being ambitious – trying to be the best in the world – and we shouldn't be afraid to aim high. I know the talent is out there but talent without opportunity comes to nothing. So we must ensure we create opportunities at every step of the way if we are to create world-class athletes.

It's not easy, but I'm one of those people who will always go out of their way to prove they can do something if other people say you can't. When I was appointed Scottish National Coach in 1995 we weren't well funded and the facilities weren't great, either. We had a tennis centre at Stirling University which had four courts and that was about it. I had no staff and a £90k budget to cover everything from talent ID to coach education and player development. But I had a lot of passion for the job and was determined to make a go of it.

I started by selecting about 20 children aged from 7-11 from all across Scotland. Out of nothing we created something special and produced four Davis Cup players and one Fed Cup player with talented youngsters like Elena Baltacha, Colin Fleming and Jamie Baker among that group. It wasn't really in line with the regular tennis world with hot-housed youngsters and crazy parents. We created a family feel, with all the parents getting involved with things like car-sharing. It was a small beginning but we created success and a lot of children fell in love with the game. I felt I was constantly battling with things like finance, but it was a big adventure. Nobody was spoilt or pampered, everyone pitched in and we got the work done.

I was determined to make us a force to be reckoned with and we did create a huge buzz, but we're in danger of failing to capitalise on it. So in 2014 I started the Tennis on the Road programme which is supported by RBS. It's basically taking a van full of equipment round the country, trying to encourage young people to play and also to build a workforce in different communities to keep driving it forward.

Not every community has tennis courts so we show them how to make the best use of whatever they have – playgrounds, school gyms, community halls or playing fields.

When we haven't been able to play outdoors we've gone into town halls and high schools – whatever it takes.

When I was a youngster it would have been just about impossible for anyone to make it in tennis on the world stage. There were hardly any indoor courts so you could only play when the weather allowed, which usually meant in the summer. Most of us who were keen on sport would play badminton in the winter. You couldn't produce international-level players against that backdrop.

Judy with her dance partner Anton du Beke

"I have the Wallace Monument on my doorstep. It's very impressive, from wherever you are standing. I love the whole Braveheart thing, and the fact that this was where he went to plan his strategy for the Battle of Stirling Bridge."

161

I first got into tennis when I was about ten, but sport was always a big part of my life. I was brought up in Stirling until I was five then we moved to Dunblane where my dad opened the first optician's practice in the high street. He had been a professional footballer and played for Stirling Albion, Hibs and Cowdenbeath. I don't remember that, but I do remember clearly that my mum and dad were always playing in the garden with me and my two younger brothers, regardless of the weather. There were always footballs, cricket stumps and goal-posts in the garden. My parents were both very active members of the tennis, badminton and golf clubs so we were always around one sport or another. You couldn't really start playing tennis any earlier than the age of ten then. Those were the days of wooden rackets and proper tennis balls, so you had to be a certain age to be able to use a racket. It's different now that you can use sponge balls, tiny rackets and mini courts.

I learned most of my tennis from Dad. You didn't have coaches for children then. He played with a lot of variety and loved doing drop shots that would go over the net and come back on the other side. He reckoned he invented the topspin forehand, long before Bjorn Borg came on the scene! He was very competitive and I think I got a lot of my character from him. Mum was completely the opposite and was a really good sport, but I wasn't one to say "good shot" to my opponent. I never saw the point because it would just encourage them to do it again.

I started competing at the age of about 11 or 12 and I just missed out on a place in the GB full-time girls squad when I was 17 so I had no option but to try and go it alone. Training in Scotland was near impossible as there were no practice partners or squads in those days. Tennis was a minority sport and there was nothing in place for anyone with ambition or potential to take the sport seriously. I had to travel overseas to find competition and, when I was playing an event in Barcelona, I had

"A choir sang Caledonia *at Andy's wedding."*

my purse stolen on a crowded bus and I was left with nothing in a foreign country where I didn't speak the language. There were no mobile phones or credit cards then – you had to have money wired to you at the post office. I had to find a way to get home and my dad said it was just too difficult so I didn't go back.

I went to Edinburgh University after that, then I worked in Glasgow. We lived in Glasgow until Andy was born then moved back to Dunblane to be closer to family. Now I live in Bridge of Allan with the Wallace Monument on my doorstep. It's very impressive, from wherever you are standing. I love the whole *Braveheart* thing, and the fact that this was where he went to plan his strategy for the Battle of Stirling Bridge. From up there you can see all round the area. If I really want to get away from it all and have total peace and quiet I go to Eriska, a tiny island near Oban. It's only about a mile and a half long, with a small hotel that used to be a country house. You go there and you're surrounded by nature and water.

I also like going to the Necropolis in Glasgow and looking at all the gravestones. You can see out to Glasgow Cathedral and the Provand's Lordship museum.

Now I spend a lot of time travelling and one of the songs that remind me of my roots is *Caledonia* which a choir sang at Andy's wedding. We have always loved that song. It makes you proud to be Scottish. I also love The Proclaimers' *500 Miles*. We always played it in the minibus when we drove the juniors to England to play tournaments and we would have a saltire flying out the window.

Ironically, putting tennis on the sidelines briefly while I was in *Strictly Come Dancing* has actually helped raise the profile of tennis in Scotland. Now when I go out on the road more people are turning up because they've seen me on the show. I didn't realise the impact it would have in terms of people recognising me. That's fine by me, if it helps deliver the tennis message.

@judmoo

"If I really want to get away from it all and have total peace and quiet I go to Eriska, a tiny island near Oban. It's only about a mile and a half long, with a small hotel that used to be a country house. You go there and you're surrounded by nature and water."
The Isle of Eriska Hotel

NICK NAIRN

chef

After leaving the Merchant Navy Nick set up his own restaurant near Aberfoyle called Braeval, *becoming the youngest Scottish chef to win a Michelin star at the age of 29. He opened a restaurant in Glasgow and cookery schools in Lake of Menteith and Aberdeen. He has appeared regularly on TV's* Ready, Steady, Cook, *presented* Landward *and was Scottish winner of* Great British Menu. *He cooked for the Queen's 80th birthday celebrations.*

HILL-WALKING AND WILD CAMPING are absolute necessities for me – I can't imagine life without that release. It's a tonic for modern living to get out into wild open spaces, and there's nowhere better than Scotland to find them. Whenever I'm grumpy, my wife packs me off into the hills with a tent and I come back restored. Just walking through the heather and bracken or down a grassy forest track speaks to my soul. We've got the most fabulous landscape out there on our doorsteps – and it's free.

The weather is another part of the whole experience. We have incredibly mixed weather. You can get four seasons in one day. It's part of the beauty of it. Some of my best days have been in blizzard conditions. You really get the sense of your own humanity and vulnerability. You are not fully in charge of your own destiny and visibility can be very low. There's nobody there to pick you up if you fall so you have to rely on yourself, and I think that's good for you.

I love the countryside. As a kid I grew up in Boquhan near Stirling which was very rural – it was a tiny village in the middle of nowhere. I have travelled all round the world with the Merchant Navy and lived in London and Glasgow, but my heart has always been in the Scottish countryside.

My grandparents lived by the Lake of Menteith and we would go there every weekend, swimming and splashing around like kids do. I remember when I was about six we would get into a rowing boat that was tethered to the jetty. Obviously we couldn't go very far, but it seemed like quite an adventure at the time. It was a real *Swallows and Amazons* existence. On the lake is the Island of Inchmahome where there's a lovely Augustine priory. Sometimes we would canoe there in the morning with the mist rising off the lake with the Trossachs in the background. I have a very strong connection to that part of Scotland. For me, nowhere else comes near.

> ❝ We were put on this planet to feed ourselves, and it's important to use the freshest ingredients

After school I spread my wings and joined the Merchant Navy. I had planned to study at Dundee University but I just didn't want to go. Instead I chose to have a few years of travel and give myself the chance to see other cultures and other things. I went to the Far East, Australia, New Zealand, India and Pakistan. I remember going to a club in Singapore and being knocked out by the food and the ambience of the place. I was just a Scottish boy and it had a real effect on me.

After that I lived in Glasgow for three years, and I have very happy memories of living in a flat in the West End. It was quite a bohemian life which gave me a taste of city living and I loved it. But when I decided to open my first restaurant I moved back to my roots.

Like everyone, I've had a lifelong interest in eating! But I was also fascinated by the whole process of sourcing good produce and making something delicious out of raw ingredients. I was self-taught and opened my first restaurant at the age of 23. Getting a Michelin star at the age of 29 was a fantastic thing, but running a restaurant really takes up most of your time and energy. It's not a recommended career if you want sensible hours and a life outside of work. It takes a lot of effort to be a leading chef and only those who have done it realise just how much. You work insane hours and you have almost to sell your soul.

Then the opportunity came up to do some television and that really took off. At one time my father Jimmy was a Scottish television announcer and he was on the *One O' Clock Gang* on STV in 1957, so I can't deny that I have showbiz in the genes.

I was surprised by the success of the showbiz side of things, though. I did three series of *Ready Steady Cook*, but I didn't expect that cooking shows would have such enduring popularity. Putting yourself on the line like that takes a lot of nerve. It's a very emotional thing. People are taken out of their comfort zones and are transported. It was an amazing experience.

Perhaps I shouldn't be so surprised that food programmes are so popular. Food and cooking touch a key part of our nature. We were put on this planet to feed ourselves. I really believe people should be able to cook: if you can't I think you are dispossessed somehow.

Seasonal and local produce is what inspires me and I think it's important to use the freshest ingredients possible. I don't know if I have a favourite dish, but an ideal meal for me would be seafood and langoustines very simply cooked with home-made mayonnaise, barbecued

"My grandparents lived by the Lake of Menteith and we would go there every weekend, swimming and splashing around like kids do. It was a real Swallows and Amazons *existence."*
The Augustine priory on Inchmahome

Aberdeen rib-eye beef with salad from the garden, triple-cooked chips and maybe one hen's egg. I would be in heaven. I also love a Glasgow roll: Ayrshire bacon and a fried egg, preferably from one of my own hens.

In the last 30 years there has been much more interest in foraging. I love the fact that food like mushrooms, wild garlic and wild sorrel is there for the taking. People are also much more aware about the importance of supporting local farmers. Our relationship with our producers is improving. As a restaurateur you have to respect the difficulties they have getting their produce into a restaurant.

We're lucky that we have the most spectacular scenery as well as fabulous produce, from the east coast right up to the western isles. It's a beautiful landscape of mountains and sky. I have two businesses in Aberdeen, which may not seem like the obvious place for what I do but it's a fascinating city. It's very wealthy in parts, and very international. I used to think it was a cold and clinical place that didn't have the warmth of Glasgow and Edinburgh, but now that I spend a lot of time in Aberdeen I have grown to love the north-east. People are harder to get to know but there is a warmth and hospitality there, almost hidden away. I love leafy enclaves in cities and Aberdeen has a few of these. I love the back wynds and the lovely old churches.

I think the reason that so many Scots succeed in life is that we think we have something to prove and we have the tenacity to do it. For me, I have Ulster Scots DNA which means I don't mind hard work. But we can be argumentative and always up for a rumble! Mixed with that, I also think we're compassionate and that we try to be more inclusive and tackle bigotry.

There are some extraordinary Scots like Sir Chris Hoy who has a drive and an extraordinary will to succeed. He has humanity and is very self-effacing, but full of confidence at the same time. Muriel Gray is another impressive Scot and she's also a good friend of mine. She is an intellectual tour de force. We spar well but she always wins. We also go hill-walking together, and she is one of the few people who walks at the same pace as me.

| nicknairn.com

| @nicknairn

"Aberdeen is a fascinating city. It's very wealthy in parts, and very international. Now that I spend a lot of time in Aberdeen I have grown to love the north-east."

DANIELA NARDINI
actress

A graduate of the Royal Scottish Academy of Music and Drama (now the Royal Conservatoire of Scotland), Daniela gained nationwide fame as Anna Forbes in BBC Two's acclaimed This Life *in the 1990s for which she won a BAFTA. She has also won two Scottish BAFTAs. She has appeared regularly on stage and in film and recently starred alongside Brian Cox in BBC's* Bob Servant.

I'M A WEST COAST GIRL at heart, and that became especially clear to me after I studied in Edinburgh for a foundation course in drama before I went to what is now the Royal Conservatoire of Scotland in Glasgow. It was good for me to live away from my family for the first time and be independent, but I never felt completely at home. The people there are different and I missed the specific humour of west coast people. There's a particular dryness and wittiness about them that I feel most comfortable with.

I was brought up in Largs and I was a child of the outdoors. I wasn't very academic so I wasn't one of those kids who stay indoors surrounded by books. I had the kind of childhood I would like my own daughter to have, forever climbing up hills, jumping from stone to stone in rivers and burns, playing rounders and constantly rushing around.

From a very young age – probably about six or seven – I knew that I loved acting. I was always putting on shows with my friends. Like most kids we enjoyed pretending to be other people – I just never stopped.

From time to time I get to see young would-be actors with my work with the Conservatoire carrying out auditions. It's quite strange because it's not always enjoyable judging people and maybe having to let them down. But it can also be great. I love it when someone comes in and has such raw talent that it just blows your mind.

I think talent is important. It's definitely true that some people have an instinct for acting while other people have to work hard at it and are more technical. The more natural ones are easier to direct because they just get it – they don't need everything to be explained to them. Maybe it's a bit like artists who have their own style and a certain feel for colour without thinking too much about the technicalities.

I'm from Italian stock – my family ran an ice-cream business – and for some reason it does seem that a lot of Scots with Italian origins move into creative areas like acting, painting and music. My family are from Braga, the same village that Paolo Nutini's family are from. I'm not saying I'm in the same league of fame as him, though! I remember opening a festival there and there were pictures of Paolo everywhere.

When my friend David McVicar (now a highy successful opera director) and I left drama school we set up a company and toured Scotland with plays and we worked closely with the poet Liz Lochhead. We went to a lot of far-flung places like Cromarty

Broughty Castle in Broughty Ferry

"One song I love is Largs by King Creosote, a musician from Perth, who wrote about the town and meeting the queen of ice-cream. It's hilarious."
Nardini's world-famous ice-cream parlour in Largs

and Plockton, sometimes playing to just a handful of people and a flock of sheep. I would be coming up to the climax of a powerful speech in *Miss Julie* or *Mary, Queen of Scots* and I'd be drowned out by the sound of a sheep going "baa"!

Going from that to *This Life* soon afterwards was quite a shock to the system. The amount of recognition was mind-boggling. It was my big break but it had

A lot of Scots with Italian origins move into creative areas like acting, painting and music

its downsides, such as people clamouring to talk to me when I was out with family and friends and just totally ignoring them. I found it so rude. On the other hand I was making good money for the first time and working with great people doing what I enjoyed. We were all young, living in London, and we adored one another. Every day was fun, so even though it was hard work it was easy in a way because we all loved it so much.

I don't think that success changed me. I'd go back to Scotland and you couldn't get away with being big-headed – no one would let you. I think that's a good thing, but we Scots can be almost a bit too modest and down on ourselves. We withhold ourselves and we aren't at all pushy. That's the case with me. I've never been pushy. I was very shy and unsure of myself for many years which might seems at odds with being in a competitive profession where people are ambitious, but a lot of actors are shy underneath it all. We just learn to live with the inevitable knocks and take them as they come.

It's great to work with people you admire such as Brian Cox, so acting alongside him in *Bob Servant* was amazing. He's a great raconteur and is very charming. He's also a man of principle who cares deeply about Scotland and he is very pro-independence. Before the referendum he kept his word and came up to give talks and walk round Dundee where he is from to spread the word.

Bob Servant was set in Broughty Ferry just outside Dundee and there was a very strong sense of place in that series. Having spent the time touring around Scotland with David McVicar I got to know places I might not have come across otherwise. I adore Plockton across from Skye and I remember a wonderful holiday in a caravan on Skye with my mum and sisters and brothers. The beaches were like white coral. I love Argyllshire and I'm also fond of Millport on the west coast. It's a special place. You could cycle round the island and then reward yourself with an ice-cream.

Ice-cream features large in my life, coming from an ice-cream dynasty. One song I love is *Largs* by King Creosote, a musician from Perth, who wrote about the town and meeting the queen of ice-cream. It's hilarious. I went to one of his concerts recently and I got someone to ask him if I was the girl in the song. I was only joking, but he didn't give a definitive answer so who knows?

"My friend David McVicar and I set up a company and toured Scotland with plays. We went to a lot of far-flung places like Cromarty, sometimes playing to just a handful of people and a flock of sheep."
View from fields to the Cromarty Firth and Dingwall

RAB NOAKES

songwriter, performer

Rab, who is still busy recording and touring, was a founder member of Stealers Wheel with Gerry Rafferty in 1971. His best-known recording is Branch *from the 1974 album* Red Pump Special, *the third of 19 solo releases to date, which was released as a 40th anniversary CD in 2014. In 1998 he became senior producer for music programmes on BBC Radio Scotland, then left in 1995 to set up his own production company Neon with wife Stephy.*

IF I HAD TO PICK ONE GREAT SCOT who has been particularly influential in my life it would have to be Hamish Imlach. He was a great performer and guitar player with a wide repertoire. He was politically aware and responsible without beating you over the head with it. While his songs could be deep and serious the introductions were invariably funny and entertaining. He had a great stagecraft, which I'd like to think I brought to my work. He had a big heart with a tremendous generosity of spirit, always happy to share his knowledge with my younger generation of performers and writers. He epitomised all that was great about that folk world.

One song that always reminds me of growing up in Scotland in the 1960s is Jeannie Robertson's *Twa Recruiting Sergeants*. I've always loved that song – great use of the Scots language. I'd be listening to it with the Vietnam War in the background, although its origins obviously lie in the shanghaiing of young men for the Napoleonic wars. It's funny, ironic, really well-written and has a strong anti-war thread, and Jeannie was an amazing performer and vocalist.

It was an interesting time growing up in Scotland after the Second World War. I was born in St Andrews in Fife and grew up in Cupar, a small market town in a farming area. We moved into a council house in 1955 and my dad worked for the Post Office as a public servant. We were the baby boomer generation. I grew up in an atmosphere of shared experience, camaraderie and equality, where public service and public housing were seen as good things. We seemed to play out in the street all day – without fear – our parents having absolutely no

idea where we were. But there was always someone looking out for you. 'Shared parenting' would be the horrible phrase you'd give it today.

We didn't have a TV until 1958 so we listened to the radio a lot. It has been a big presence in my life from the early days of listening to pop music like The Beatles to becoming senior producer for music programmes at Radio Scotland later in life, in 1988. There's a certain symmetry there – everything comes full circle. In those days you had to go hunting for pop, though. It's the old cliché of listening to Radio Luxembourg on a transistor under the bed covers – but it was true.

> ## " In Glasgow I saw all the best groups for five bob in the cheap seats

I have two younger brothers, Alan and Ken, and we would take our holidays visiting cousins, aunts and uncles in north Fife and Dundee. In 1958 we also got our first family car – a 1933 Rover 10 – and it took us everywhere. We're only talking about travelling 30 or 40 miles up the road but it seemed like a massive adventure to us. I also vividly remember a fortnight's summer holiday in 1962 where I cycled with my pal Geoff Alexander right round Scotland up to Perthshire, across to Skye, up to Inverness and back via Deeside and Aberdeen home down the east coast, staying in youth hostels along the way.

My mum was a really good singer so there was a lot of singing in the house and I could always sing. On the radio you'd hear things like The Weavers doing *So Long, It's Been Good to Know You*. Songs like that still resonate with me today and Scottish things like Robert Wilson's *A Gordon For Me*. Early folk influences would be Robin Hall and Jimmie Macgregor on the *Tonight* programme or *White Heather Club* or the Joe Gordon Folk Four. I started to play guitar at school aged 11 or 12 but I didn't have my own until I was about 15. We were self-taught. Friends would show you things and you listened to records and worked out chords. You'd read the Melody Maker and find John Lennon saying: "You've got to listen to Bob Dylan." You check that out and find he is another gatekeeper and it leads you to Woody Guthrie, then you'd realise you'd already heard him through Lonnie Donegan and skiffle. There's a certain archaeology and lineage there. And for me it was always about singing and songwriting rather than being the master of an instrument.

I left school at 16 in 1963 and went to work in Glasgow for the Civil Service. It wasn't the desire to get away from somewhere small and stifling: that's where the jobs were. It was an exciting place to be as a teenager. The mod fashions were emerging. I went to all the pop shows at the Odeon cinema in Renfield Street. I saw all the best groups for five bob in the cheap seats. London was already beckoning but I wouldn't be there until 1966. I met Gerry Rafferty in 1969 when The Humblebums did a concert at Glasgow City Hall. We would form Stealers Wheel in 1971. It was around the same time I met

Lindisfarne, who were called Brethren then. Mrs Fisher used to run a folk club at the Duke of York in Wallsend and we both played there. We were all about the same age, kindred spirits, and we got on from the word go. It was starting a voyage of discovery and getting more involved in folk and all its riches. It was a tremendous education.

There are a couple of great vistas in Glasgow that I love: from the flagpole promontories in Ruchill Park looking south and in Queen's Park looking north across the city. I still live in Glasgow. I came back again after living in London and Manchester when I got the Radio Scotland job. I've always felt this is home but I would say that I'm not thirled to the idea of location being terribly significant. I have always felt my lifespan to have exercised more influence than location, particularly the way the world has shrunk in the past 60 years. But I do love the way the city changes. It's a landscape that's constantly changing. I can spend ages looking at aerial photographs, picking out particular buildings. It's nice to see familiar places like the Central Station – which you might see every day – from a totally different perspective. Another vista that intrigues me is the view of all the three bridges over the Forth as the new Queensferry Crossing is being constructed. I find that quite exciting because I remember as a young man travelling by train in 1964 when the Forth Road Bridge was just coming to life. And it's nice to see the third one coming to life now.

rabnoakes.com

"A vista that intrigues me is the view of all the three bridges over the Forth as the new Queensferry Crossing is being constructed. I find that quite exciting because I remember as a young man travelling by train in 1964 when the Forth Road Bridge was just coming to life. And it's nice to see the third one coming to life now."

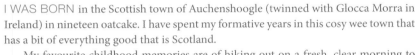

OOR WULLIE
Scotland's favourite son

Oor Wullie is the iconic character in the cartoon strip that bears his name in the Sunday Post newspaper. He is best known for leading his gang of fellow youngsters into mischief – and for using a bucket as a seat.

I WAS BORN in the Scottish town of Auchenshoogle (twinned with Glocca Morra in Ireland) in nineteen oatcake. I have spent my formative years in this cosy wee town that has a bit of everything good that is Scotland.

My favourite childhood memories are of hiking out on a fresh, clear morning to go camping wi' my pals amongst the heather and hills of Stoorie Brae, just a short way from my home. It never dampened our spirits if it was raining; it was just so good to be out on an adventure. We fried trout we caught in the burns and feasted on brambles, blaeberries and tiny sweet wild rasps. We were all budding Bear Gryllses back then. Though, if truth be told, we also took from home a great pile of sandwiches, scones and pancakes to give us energy to climb the hills and wander the miles of forest paths. Everything seemed to taste better out in the open air. The local policeman, PC Murdoch, would keep an eye on us to see we were not getting into mischief, but really he was just making sure we were safe. He also brought his fishing rod, tied to the bar of his police bicycle, and enjoyed casting a fly to see if he could out-fish us. Murdoch was a grand policeman but he never arrested many trout.

During the school holidays Ma and Pa would take me to the seaside at weekends. If the weather was bonny we would go tae Ayrshire to spend hours on the sands. My favourite was to visit Culzean Castle and then go down to Croy Beach at Maybole. I got my bucket and spade and tried to recreate Culzean Castle in sand. I would get one turret done and a flag in it before the tide came in to wash it flat. If we had been at the Viking centre in Largs I would be a Viking warrior wading ashore from my Longboat to plunder Ma's picnic basket. Ma would become a berserker if I got sand on her jeely pieces. If Pa went to play golf and Ma fell asleep under her beach umbrella there was always other kids to play with – it was such a good beach.

My most favouritist trip would take us further from home up into the West Highland coast. It is a little-known fact that I am a great scientist and guddling about in the rock pools of the sea lochs up there, I learnt loads. Very few people know that a starfish can climb out your bucket in about thirty seconds – but I do. I wrote educational papers about my holidays when I went back to school but all the teacher said was that Fort William was never called Fort Wullie. Huh! What does she know.

Everyone knows that I like fun, and liking fun and laughter is one of the special

Culzean Castle which Oor Wullie tried to recreate in sand

"My most favouritist trip would take us into the West Highland coast. I wrote educational papers about my holidays when I went back to school but all the teacher said was that Fort William was never called Fort Wullie."
Fort William with Ben Nevis in the background

things I admire about us Scots. Best of all is the way we laugh at ourselves and tell stories about how mean we are. Do you know why Pa fitted double-glazing to our house? So that I couldn't hear the ice-cream van chimes. That sort of stuff. PC Murdoch writes about some of my funniest moments in his police notebook but Ma and Pa never seem to laugh at them.

Two of my favourite places to visit in Scotland are the Wallace Monument at Stirling and Loch Ness. I like to climb to the top of Wallace Monument and imagine the great battles that took place nearby. I bet that Sir William Wallace was known to his pals as Wullie too. I thought he was a giant because his sword was that huge but when the movie *Braveheart* came out he was not that tall after all – and he had an Australian accent.

When I visit Loch Ness it's usually with adults that go on about the stunning scenery but I'm not looking at the hills and glens – I'm looking in the water for the Loch Ness monster – known to us as Nessie. Legend says it is a prehistoric beastie and I try to catch it every visit. I tied a sausage on my line last trip but my friend Primrose Patterson said it is probably a vegetarian. So I tied a deep-fried Mars bar to my line instead but still no luck.

If I was asked to describe the Scots I would say they are entertaining – in every way. From Andy Murray's world-class tennis to Sean Connery's classic James Bond to Erchie Boag juggling turnips at the Huntly Show. We're entertainers every one.

Personally I was greatly inspired by Scots in space. First Ewan McGregor who saved the universe in *Star Wars* then David Tennant and Peter Capaldi who zipped around in the Tardis as Doctor Who. I've imagined my shed was a Tardis often and even Ma said the mess it is in is out of this world. Probably the most talented Scot ever was Mr Tunnock who invented the legendary teacake.

If I had come up with that recipe I wouldn't have told anybody and just got Ma to make them and scoffed every one myself. I have a high regard also for the film megastar Alan Cumming. Him and I are buddies and he wears a suit made from my Oor Wullie tartan – it's a braw bright tartan!

There are many moments in my life that I am proud of – not coming last in an arithmetic test one year. Being mascot for Scotland Rugby Sevens team. Making a CD of my favourite tunes and it got into the charts. Escorting Lorraine Kelly to collect her MBE. Being in the opening ceremony of the Commonwealth Games in Glasgow. However, the thing I am most proud about is a very Scottish thing – it is having and keeping my true friends Fat Bob and Soapy Soutar through many, many years and all the ups and downs life throws at a Scottish laddie.

Oor Wullie® © DC Thomson & Co. Ltd. 2015

"When I visit Loch Ness it's usually with adults that go on about the stunning scenery but I'm not looking at the hills and glens – I'm looking in the water for the Loch Ness monster – known to us as Nessie."
Urquhart Castle on Loch Ness

BILL PATERSON
actor

After an acting debut in 1967 in the Resistible Rise of Arturo Ui *starring Leonard Rossiter at the Citizens Theatre in Glasgow, Bill has enjoyed a distinguished stage, film and TV career.*
His films include Miss Potter, Comfort and Joy, The Witches, A Private Function *and* The Killing Fields *and his TV work includes* Auf Wiedersehen, Pet, The Singing Detective, Sea of Souls, The Crow Road *and* Outlander. *In 2015 he returned to the Scottish stage in* Waiting for Godot *with Brian Cox.*

THE SOUND OF THE TRAMS was the soundtrack of our lives. The last trams in our street ran past our close in the last month of the last year of the 1950s and it sealed the lid on my childhood. I slept in the front room above the street, and I developed an almost psychic ability to tell which route number was passing just by screwing up my eyes and listening hard. I would make bets with myself and then run to the window to see if I was right – and I usually was. There were only two routes to choose from – the 6 and the 8. The 7 we only heard. We never saw. The 6 could take you to the far western shipyards of Scotstoun via Sauchiehall Street and Kelvingrove and the 8 crawled down Renfield Street and way, way on through the Gorbals and Eglinton Toll to Rouken Glen – so beautiful but so distant that it seemed to be almost in Ireland.

When we jumped on the tram we raced each other up the stairs to 'bags' the wee compartments at the front or back. These wee cabins had their own sliding door and gave the impression you were travelling first class wherever you went – at no extra charge. And wherever we went it was, nine times out of ten, the Art Galleries. Like most kids who cruised the tramlines of north Glasgow we were like homing pigeons when it came to the Art Galleries at Kelvingrove. But it certainly wasn't to look at the paintings. They were upstairs and we never got further than the ground floor, especially the ship models and the stuffed elephants from Calderpark Zoo. It was because it was the one free, spectacular place where you could get a sense of just how big our city really was. You could stare at other Glasgow kids who lived

in unbelievably exotic places like Shawlands and Partick. They didn't know us and we didn't know them. Quite the reverse of the back green.

For as long as anyone could recall our communal half-acre was known as the back green – although there were rumours that in other parts of the city they were known as back courts. Neither name came anywhere close to describing those tight oblongs of beaten earth created by five storeys of sandstone cliffs – the tenement blocks of Dennistoun.

And kicking a ball was the first and probably last thing we all did. Beyond were the waste grounds, streets and cinder football pitches of Glasgow where you breathed in football with the very soot and stoor of the city. Where not to have an opinion on the game was the same as not having a right leg. And of the half-dozen Glasgow clubs we could support by the far the nearest to the back green was Celtic Park at Parkhead – or Paradise as it was known. So near that when the wind blew from the south-east on a Saturday afternoon you could tell when Celtic had scored – a swelling, rumbling surge like a giant clearing his throat.

Just because they were our nearest team didn't mean we could support them, of course. We were from the other side of that blue/green divide that split the city like a crevasse. Instead of a walk to Paradise with the green-and-white hordes that passed our close, we had to ride on a tram into town and travel seven stops on the underground to reach our alleged Valhalla at Ibrox Park. "There'll be sad hearts in the Vatican tonight," was the poetic image conjured up when Rangers did well or

Celtic did badly. But the love affair came to a violent end one Saturday when we saw an ugly and bloody melee outside Ibrox Park and my dad said: "Never again."

We switched our allegiance back to an old family tradition and started to support Third Lanark in the south side of the city. For some reason they were better known as the Hi-Hi. But in the 1950s that didn't describe their position in the Scottish League. A few years later they were gone but their wee ground Cathkin Park is still there – minus its rickety old stand.

Childhood Saturdays were epitomised by the Bowery Boys and Abbott and Costello at the Gaumont picture house. But it's almost impossible now to imagine the serene silence and emptiness of a Scottish Sunday in the 1950s. No one – but no one – was in the back green or kicked a ball. The Church of Scotland went through our lives like the lettering on a stick of rock and it was behind almost everything we did. My dad was a Session Clerk at St. George's Tron. Although he took it very seriously my folks had a low tolerance for what they called the 'Holy Rollers.' Very little Bible-bashing went on in our house, but a lot of tea-making.

Every summer I still get a yearning to visit the Isle of Cumbrae, a slice of Ayrshire bathing in the rich waters of the Firth of Clyde. It has a bit of Mull and Islay about it, the tiniest hint of Tiree and Barra. But it also had a couthy little Victorian town called Millport wrapped round a couple of sandy bays dotted with islands and rocks. For 20 years we spent the whole month of August in a wee rented house somewhere on the front at Millport. In the 1950s it was a children's paradise because there

"There was always something lonely and wild at this spot just around Portachur Point from the West Bay. The dark volcanic rocks, the reddish shingle and the wonderful view of Arran make it almost Hebridean – and it's only 30 miles by seagull from Sauchiehall Street!"
Great Cumbrae Island

With Brian Cox in Waiting for Godot

juke box. No wonder a single Chuck Berry chord still has a direct line to that Millport mood.

In 1962 my two Damascene roads were only 20 miles apart but they were as different as could be. One was the A809 heading north over the Stockiemuir Road to Drymen opening out to a view of the whole of the southern Highlands. Rock climbing on the Whangie – a canyon of rock split off the side of Auchineden Hill – was a great way to spend a Sunday with my pal Gordon. And although I started with 'E' for easy and worked my way sideways, I knew this airy risky place with great views to the north was going to be the start of a teenage crush on Scotland's wilder places that would last forever. Ben Lomond and the Arrochar Alps and the great mountains of Glencoe beckoned.

Meanwhile I had started to take the trolley bus to the Citizens Theatre at Gorbals Cross – where the old A8 met the old A74. The upper circle became my second home after John Swan, my excellent English teacher, had dragged me and 30 other reluctant teenagers to see *A Man For All Seasons* there. It wasn't just the plays. It was everything about this magical place. The smell of the scenery and the greasepaint mixing with the distant whiff of the chippy next door and the coffee from the wee tea-room in the foyer. It was a heady mixture and I was addicted. I joined the Young Citz Society and you could see a show for 9d. I left school and became an apprentice quantity surveyor but they kindly let me go and I crept in under the door of the College of Drama and began the wandering life that took me away forever from the back green.

Reproduced by kind permission of Bill Paterson from his radio series *Tales from the Back Green*

were more vehicles in a Glasgow car showroom than on the whole of the Cumbrae. Bicycles on the island outnumbered people by about three to one. For fifteen shillings Frank Mapes would rent you one for a month from his fantastic shop. No strings except Frank's eleventh commandment: Thou Shalt Not Take Bikes on the Sand.

Childhood passed. But before becoming adults we could try this new thing from America called being a teenager. If you had to be a teenager in Scotland in the late 1950s you could do a lot worse than Millport in August. It had a little whiff of Coney Island. That Millport freedom was even sweeter when Elvis was on the juke box in Andy's Snack Bar at the Garrison. He ran a great

"Ben Lomond and the Arrochar Alps and the great mountains of Glencoe beckoned."
Ben Lomond in the autumn mist

183

GAIL PORTER
TV presenter and model

As well as presenting a range of television shows including Top of the Pops, Live and Kicking *and* The Big Breakfast, *Gail was also a successful model. An image of her naked was projected onto the Houses of Parliament by FHM magazine in 1999. More recently she has been writing autobiographical work. Gail actively supports charities and is vice-president of The Children's Trust.*

SCOTLAND IS MY HOME although I live in London, and I've told my daughter that I'd love to go back as soon as she has finished school. On a recent trip to Glasgow with my boyfriend we went out to Loch Lomond and it was just the nicest thing. We sat down and looked out onto the water and it was lovely. I felt like a salmon who had gone back to its home river. When I'm in Scotland it makes me feel like I'm learning to breathe again. I have a friend who lives in Arran and it is beautiful there. When I go to see her I like to have a swim in the sea, whatever the time of year. People may think it's crazy but I'm Scottish – it's what we do!

I was born in Edinburgh in the Simpson Memorial Hospital in 1971 and I have a younger brother, Keith. We lived in Portobello in Edinburgh and my dad is still there. I lost my mum when she was 60. We were the family that went to Portobello and never left. Even when my parents split up, we didn't move from Portobello.

We were never a wealthy family so we didn't travel far for our holidays, but I have some great memories of going to stay at a little place which had lodges near Aviemore where we'd go as children. It was so much fun.

When we were little my brother and I were always making stuff up. We would go outside on our Chopper bikes and pretend we were *The Professionals* from the TV show. We had pretend walkie-talkies and always spoke, for some reason, in American accents! We were best friends. My brother and I also used to do Highland dancing, especially at Hogmanay when we'd go round the doors in the neighbourhood.

When I wasn't being a *Professional* I used to spend my time in the library. I was the kid at school who always

Aviemore and surrounding countryside

had her hand up first in class, even before the teacher would ask a question. I was a bit of a loner and I wanted everyone to think I was clever. My nickname was Snobby Porter. I wanted to go home and be able to tell my mum I had the best grades in class, to try to impress her.

My parents handled their separation very well. I had lots of friends who had parents who got divorced and they found it hard. For me, at the time, I couldn't see why. It wasn't a big issue for me. I had two people who loved me, who were always there for me, and I had two birthdays and two Christmases every year!

I think Scotland is one of the most special places in the world, ever. Every time I arrive into Glasgow on the train there is something that lifts my heart and I am so incredibly happy. It's the people, 100 per cent. They smile and say: "All right, Gail?" and I feel I'm where I belong.

185

You can be yourself and just strike up a conversation with anyone. Sometimes when I get on the Tube in London and I smile at people they look at me as if I'm insane.

There are places that make you remember people so deeply that it hurts. I feel this particularly in Edinburgh. I miss my mum like crazy. Every year we would walk to the Edinburgh Festival and Mum would insist on going to her favourite fish and chip shop on the Royal Mile. No other one would do. Those were the chips she wanted. Even though my daughter was born in England I bring her up to Scotland all the time and she thinks it's amazing. When we go to the festival she thinks it's magical. I've always enjoyed music and festivals, and one of my favourite bands is The Red Hot Chilli Pipers who I saw at a festival in Glasgow. I am massively into bagpipes and these pipers are brilliant. They do everything from Queen to Adele and they're very tongue-in-cheek.

When I got my first job on television it was by fluke. I was working behind the scenes and someone offered me an audition for an interactive game show. Mum went: "Just go for it," but she never really seemed as impressed by it as my nan was when I got the job. Nan was so excited and was so proud of me. I was pleased for myself, too. I was never bothered about the money – it was just great fun and of course it led on to other things so it gave me a great start in showbusiness.

Dad never made a big thing of it. He would say: "Whatever. Now, do you want some fish fingers for your tea?" It's a very Scottish way of handling things, and having someone like that in your life keeps you grounded. It also means I am never really fazed by anything because I've never been allowed to take myself too seriously.

My presenting career was good fun, but nowadays I'm much more interested in writing, and I get my inspiration from brilliant writers like Irvine Welsh. When I first read *Trainspotting* I thought it was unbelievable. I was fascinated at how he could tackle such a tough subject as drug addiction and still get comedy out of it. His books make me laugh out loud and I have huge respect for him. I went to the launch of one of his books and we met there. I was trying to be really cool but I failed about 100 per cent. Now we have become friends.

I'm writing an autobiography and I wondered how I would tackle some of the harder times in my life. I was sectioned a long time ago and wondered whether I should write about that experience. Irvine said I should just do it and use what happened to me in my work. If, by writing about it, I can help someone else who has had depression it will make me happy. If some people don't like what I write, that's up to them. I really don't care what other people think these days. I deal with my problems now by running. I don't always enjoy it but I run every day and feel so much better afterwards. It works for me. I just run and run – like Forrest Gump!

@gailporter

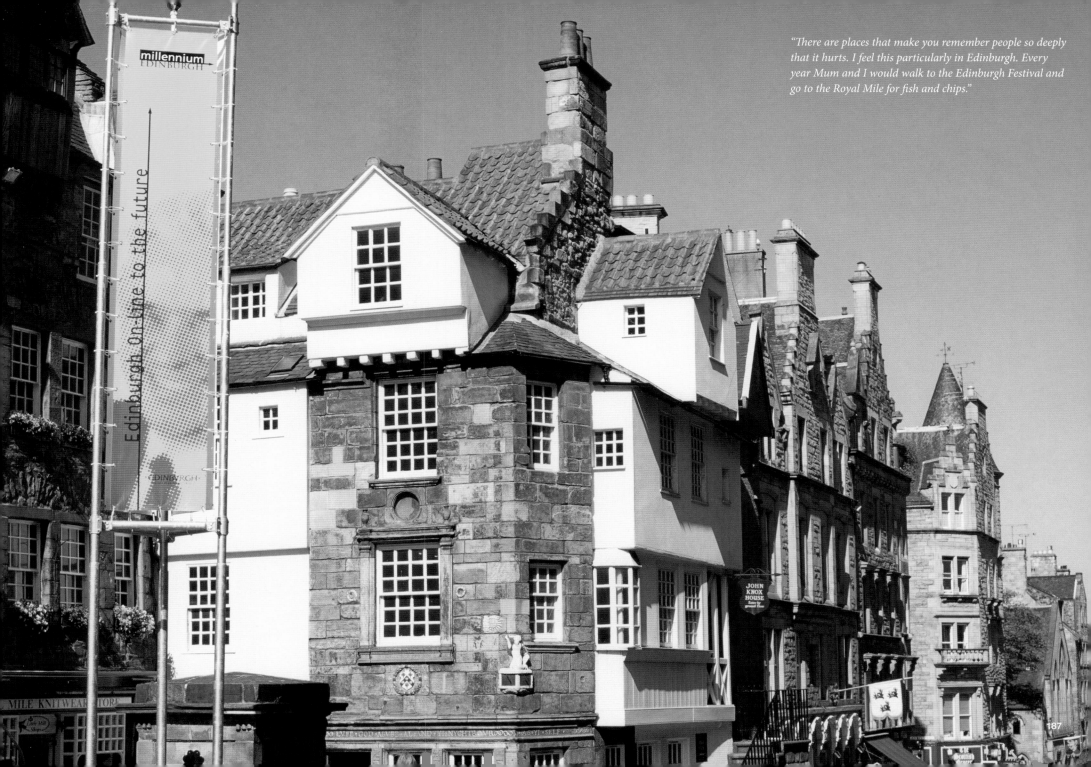

"*There are places that make you remember people so deeply that it hurts. I feel this particularly in Edinburgh. Every year Mum and I would walk to the Edinburgh Festival and go to the Royal Mile for fish and chips.*"

EDDI READER MBE

singer-songwriter

Since fronting the 1980s band Fairground Attraction, Eddi has also enjoyed an enduring solo career. She has received three BRIT awards and topped both the singles and album charts. In 2003 she showcased the works of Robert Burns and was awarded an MBE in 2006 for outstanding contributions to the arts.

I WAS BORN AND BROUGHT UP in the Anderson tenements for the first five or six years of my life, then Arden council estate for ten years. After that we were deported from Glasgow to Irvine in Ayrshire but I stayed during the week at my gran's in Pollok until the end of compulsory school. Then I had another two school years in Irvine before hitting the road at 18. I never had a plan. I just aligned myself to songs I liked and started busking.

I particularly admire the Glasgow women who moved with us to Irvine and began a community drop-in for the older people who were moved out of Glasgow and others who felt isolated. They have been serving them for 40 years now completely voluntarily.

I think one of my proudest moments came when the drop-in was threatened with closure through lack of funds. The council wanted impersonal home helps to replace the drop-in charity service. It was a difficult time and most of the pensioners were devastated that they would lose their place. But the Queen stepped in and awarded the drop-in a Silver Jubilee award and that made the highheidyins back off. They have been going strong ever since, but they still need funding and people to help out.

The balustrades in the Glasgow buildings are one of my earliest memories. I might have lived in what was called slums but I thought they were castle walls. It was the early 1960s and the tenement buildings were cheap housing for the workers and their wives and kids. They were big stone buildings with china walls or china tiles around the walls, and they were great for singing in.

And the kids – me and my sisters and brothers, everyone – all the children in the area, we would have to

"I would spend every weekend up at the Kelvingrove Art Gallery."

188

"One very special holiday when I was 13 was in Islay. I have remembered its beauty all my life." Portnahaven in Islay

189

wash the walls and the stairs down. We got a couple of pennies for doing it. That's where I started singing because we didn't really have a big enough bathroom for

> ## " I always loved to sing and I do have some musical DNA

me to hog it. I would wash the stairs. It sounds very romantic and Edith Piaf, sort of washing the stairs and singing my songs. I can't remember what I used to sing. I think I just used to improvise and go la, la, la. I always loved to sing.

I do have some musical DNA. I discovered my great-great-great-grandad was a German busking musical instrument maker and my great-grandad – his grandson – liked to sing Robert Burns and traditional Scots songs as a hobby. That's my dad's side. Then my mum has a very sweet singing voice. She was known in the family as the singer. Mum sang like Doris Day and Dad was a real Elvis freak so I did a lot of *Crying in the Chapel* and *Are You Lonesome Tonight?* – that was the one I sang! We were working class, and that was the way that we entertained ourselves. Everyone thinks that they're a singer in Glasgow. Everyone had their song, and you couldn't sing that person's song. So Auntie Mary had hers, Uncle Frank had his Frank Sinatra, Uncle Terrence had his Dean Martin song, Auntie Marion had her Beatles song.

It was a real education in pop culture for me, being with these grown-ups. All my family influenced me.

My most vivid childhood memories of Scotland are the seemingly endless summers and rainy days, family parties and babysitting, running errands or, as we call them, messages. My dad would drive us all over the west of Scotland and up the hilly roads that sent us all flying in the back seat. He worked away and came home with talk of exotic places like Skye and the very north of Scotland – and how beautiful it was. Formal holidays would be a rented house or couple of rooms, mostly in Saltcoats.

One time we went east to London Links, and one very special holiday when I was 13 was in Islay. I have remembered its beauty all my life. We rented a big house. There were six of us kids and another one on the way the next year. I was becoming a woman and I was deeply affected by the nature around me. I also ADORE the view from Irvine Beach out to Arran island. Many dreams of mine took flight from that spot.

I love the top of Buchanan Street and the sight all the way down into the heart of Glasgow's valley. It always looks dramatic on a sunny afternoon. I love to imagine the millions of lives that have lived and worked and loved there and passed the city on to the next generation.

When I fancied myself as a famous but troubled artist in my teens I would spend every weekend up at Kelvingrove Art Gallery sketching the *Fishermen's Wives* or gazing at the *Crucifixion* by Dali or desperately looking for clues in the exhibitions of ancient ballroom gowns fully displayed with their gloves and little dance books!

Scotland is special to me because it's my home and it has everything I need to feel safe and loved. And the Scottish people, of course – kind-hearted, worried for each other, supportive but quick to snap you back to earth if you fly too high up your own arse.

eddireader.co.uk

"I love the top of Buchanan Street and the sight all the way down into the heart of Glasgow's valley. It always looks dramatic on a sunny afternoon. I love to imagine the millions of lives that have lived and worked and loved there and passed the city on to the next generation."

JEAN REDPATH MBE 1937-2014

traditional singer

Celebrated as one of the greatest Scottish traditional singers, Jean spread the gospel across the world and particularly in America, where she lived from 1961. Born and bred in Fife, Jean – who died in America in August 2014 at the age of 77 – had produced over 40 albums and in 1987 was made an MBE in the Queen's Birthday Honours. This was one of Jean's final interviews before her death.

SINGING ISN'T A REAL JOB and at the outset I certainly had no notion of earning a living with my voice.

My parents, Jim and Isabella (known as Bluebell), were both quite musical so it was no surprise that I found myself absorbing an enormous amount at home in Leven, Fife. My dad taught himself to play the hammer dulcimer and had both a fine voice and terminal shyness; my mother had a vast repertoire of everything from bothy ballads to bawdery and Victorian parlour songs.

None of this was music, of course, as I quickly learned when I went to school. Hopefully mine was the last generation to be persuaded that only English art songs were fit to sing. But a career in Scottish traditional song? Surely that had to be a jest.

My mother was one of 12 siblings, my father one of three, so there were many sources of reference if the odd verse was forgotten. Nearly all of the family stayed in Fife, naturally. The older generation is gone now, but my brother and his wife still live close by and there are many cousins and their offspring in the Kingdom.

I have lived in America for over half a century since emigrating there aged 24 in March 1961, and have commuted for the same length of time, sometimes several times a year, performing on both sides of the Atlantic. For me, home is where the suitcase is.

From my parents I inherited a love of the country, although my father favoured the Borders and the more tailored roads of southern Scotland, and my mother preferred the wildness of the north and west. This is hardly surprising: the village of Redpath is in the Borders and my mother's folk came from Brora in the north.

"The first glimpse of Largo Law brings a lift to my heart and a smile to my face. When I see it, I know I'm home." Largo and Largo Law from near Ruddon Point

193

For me, it's the first glimpse of Largo Law that brings a lift to my heart and a smile to my face. When I see it, I know I'm home.

It's our local 'mountain', not quite 1,000ft high and a breathless climb with a glorious view, particularly of the Firth of Forth and a' the lands aboot it. There's Edinburgh, my birthplace, to the south-west, the Bass Rock and its 150,000 gannets across the water, and to the east the Isle of May, with 120,000 puffins. A bird-watcher's heaven.

I always gravitate back to the sea eventually, but the village of Falkland inland has had a strong attraction, and the East Falkland Hill is a lot easier to climb these days. There's a car park up near its base which has yet another magnificent view.

" We all need tap-roots – they rebuild our sense of purpose

And then there's St Andrews, of which I saw a good deal as a teenager. Who can explain the spell cast by some places and buildings? The strongest feeling inspired by the martyrs' crosses and the ruins of St Andrews Cathedral, as by the shells of the Border abbeys, is disbelief in the violence and idiocy of religious fanaticism. No wonder the Scots sing! How else would they have survived?

The name of Robert Burns must have come up in high school, but I have little recollection of any of his work apart from one song, *Tae the Weaver's Gin Ye Go*, which was taught and delivered in the stiff, unnatural and painfully articulated manner that inspired such self-consciousness.

Not until Hamish Henderson's talk to the Literary Society and my discovery of the Edinburgh University Folk Song Society did I become aware of traditional music, traditional singers and a whole world of oral tradition beyond my mother's kitchen and living room. The School of Scottish Studies was an Aladdin's Cave and Hamish a gold mine of information and encouragement.

It was through Hamish that, many years later, I met Serge Hovey, that remarkable man with whom I spent 20 years recording 180 songs of Robert Burns, most of which I had never heard or had never associated with Burns.

Leaving Scotland for the USA in 1961 was nothing as well-considered as a career move. From this vantage point I see it as a delayed teenage rebellion, a flexing of wings, a gap year that turned out to last for half a century.

Twenty-four is well within the immortal and indestructible years when flying 6,000 miles with only a plane ticket and a fiver in the pocket did not seem daunting. Nowhere in the months before, or the six months after I landed in California, was singing a factor. Graduating from casual labour to wandering minstrel was unplanned, serendipitous, and again thanks to Hamish Henderson's influence in the wings.

I left the shelter of the friends' farm in northern California, stumbled into the folk music revival in New York, and rubbed shoulders with a very young Bob Dylan, with Dave van Ronk, with Jack Elliot and with most of the performers who passed through Greenwich Village in the 1960s. It must have been nearly ten years after that when I realised that this was what I was doing for a living and for the love of it: there was never any carefully considered career path.

The one constant in this peripatetic existence, and a great strength in working in a very specialised area, was the fact that I never doubted for a second the value of the material I was presenting, nor the belief that everyone should visit Scotland at least twice.

In the early days it was discouraging to be asked for *I Belong to Glasgow*, or *Loch Lomond*, but if such repertoire was what was taught in schools, I could understand – and do my best to expand those musical horizons.

Was this a mission? Oh, heavens no, I don't think so. There was just so much powerful and beautiful song available, why would one settle for less? The honours that came through the years were always somewhat of a surprise. I have been privileged to spend my life travelling and doing something I love: public and academic recognition are a huge bonus.

Returning to Edinburgh University and the School of Celtic and Scottish Studies was thrilling, mostly because here was evidence that young people were still interested in their own culture and language.

Scotland is one of those countries that inspire fierce loyalty, nostalgia, and – in its exiles – the need to go 'home' whenever possible. I have been lucky in commuting across the Atlantic for many years and re-connecting with my personal tap-root in Fife. We all need tap-roots; they give us strength, they rebuild our sense of purpose and for me this was best expressed by the Bard himself:

Ev'n then, a wish, (I mind its power)
A wish, that, to my latest hour,
Shall strongly heave my breast;
That I for poor auld Scotland's sake
Some useful plan, or book could make,
Or sing a sang at least.
From *Epistle to Mrs Scott, or the Answer to the Guidwife of Wauchope-House*. Robert Burns, 1787

Much quoted it may be, but it says it all for me!

"And then there's St Andrews, of which I saw a good deal as a teenager. Who can explain the spell cast by some places and buildings?"

195

JAMES ROBERTSON
writer

James Robertson is a poet and novelist. His novels include Joseph Knight, And the Land Lay Still *(both winners of the Saltire Society Book of the Year award),* The Testament of Gideon Mack *and* The Professor of Truth. *He also writes and edits books in Scots for young readers under the Itchy Coo imprint, and has translated classics such as* Winnie-the-Pooh *and* The Gruffalo *into Scots.*

I FELT COMPLETELY SCOTTISH from an early age, even though I was born in Sevenoaks in Kent and both of my parents were born in England. But three of my grandparents were Scottish – with ancestry in the Highlands on my father's side – so there was always a connection. We moved from Kent in 1964 when my father got a job in Scotland. I was six at the time, and it would be 35 years before I'd revisit Sevenoaks.

We went to live in Bridge of Allan which was quite well-to-do and middle-class. It was a quiet and beautiful place in which to grow up. Although it was close to Stirling it was a separate village in those days: now it's become almost a suburb, with the university, which opened in 1967, having filled in much of the space between them. The great thing about the village was that I could get on my bicycle and, only five minutes from the house, I'd be in wonderful, open countryside. It felt completely safe and I was given free rein to explore.

Unlike most Scottish people I was educated privately. This has left me with a strong antipathy to private education. From the age of seven to 13 I went to a prep school in Stirling and I was quite conscious that I was privileged and that it marked me out as slightly different in and around where we lived. Looking back, though, the school itself was very good. Later I went to board at Glenalmond College in Perthshire which was much more elitist, modelled on the English public school system. The most accurate thing to say is that I survived it. I didn't hate it but I didn't love it either. There was just something about it that rankled. The opportunities it offered in terms of outdoor activities and sports were

Stirling Castle

"The landscape of my childhood takes in historical locations like Stirling Castle and the Wallace Monument as well as the hills of the southern Highlands."

good, and I quite enjoyed these, but for kids who didn't it must have been a nightmare.

Scotland has a strong sense of itself as egalitarian and democratic, which is one reason why Robert Burns is so revered – because of those aspirations in his work. If some of the class division associated with private education is not so widespread or visible in Scotland as it is in England, it is certainly there.

When people talk about the Scottish national character I am a bit wary. I think it's dangerous and misleading to assume everyone is the same. One of the interesting things about Scotland in the last 30 to 40 years is how we have successfully managed to break away from some of the old stereotypes of what it is to be Scottish. Actually Scotland is a very diverse country.

If you live on an island, for example, you are bound to have a different outlook to someone who is from a city. A third of the population live in communities of 10,000 inhabitants or fewer. Ethnically and culturally Scotland is far more varied than it was when I was a child. Sectarianism is still a problem in some parts of the country, but your faith background is less important today than was once the case – we have become a largely secular society. Most of us are less defined by religion than older generations, and on the whole that's a good thing. That's one of the themes of my novel *The Testament of Gideon Mack*. On the other hand, when things change you often lose something. When I grew up Sundays were quieter and gentler, and in that sense special, whereas now they're just like any other day.

In the same vein, a lot of our communities have changed or broken down because of the loss of certain industries and associated jobs and that has diminished the quality and value of many people's lives. There was a cohesion to these communities that has been destroyed.

One thing that strikes me about Scotland that does remain constant is that, even if you live in the middle of Glasgow or Edinburgh or Aberdeen it doesn't take very long to get out of the city. You can look from the city

and see hills and open spaces and a landscape that is not urban at all. Metaphorically, if not practically, that offers everyone a sense of broadening horizons, of liberation from possibly straitened circumstances. Many Scots have a very strong belief in the right to roam, to have free access to what they see as their land – no matter whose name is on the title deeds.

I definitely feel that. I hadn't actually been outside the British Isles until I was 20 because we would always take our holidays here – usually in the Highlands though sometimes in England and once in Ireland. My father's ancestors are from Easter Ross and we used to go up there and explore where he had come from. We used to rent holiday cottages in Sutherland, in the Dornoch area, and eventually my parents retired and settled there.

The landscape of my childhood takes in historical locations like Stirling Castle and the Wallace Monument as well as the hills of the southern Highlands. I've heard people say that my books often seem to be inspired by the places where I happen to be at the time of writing them. That wasn't intentional but I think it's largely true.

I now live in Angus about ten miles north of Dundee and my favourite place is there, in the ancient territory of the Picts. The Picts left lots of standing stones and there is one of these about two miles from where I live. From that place you get the most magnificent view of the southern Grampians spread out before you. In the spring the hills are still covered with snow and it's just gorgeous. You can see a landscape that hasn't changed much for hundreds of years.

Another hugely important aspect of Scotland's culture is music. We have a huge repertoire of songs and tunes, both modern and traditional, that we can be really proud of. One that always moves me is *Hermless* by my friend Michael Marra, who died in 2012. It is the least aggressive song you will ever hear, and many people think of it as an alternative Scottish national anthem. Another song I love is *Follow the Heron* by Karine Polwart. The heron is a bird that to me signifies patience, resilience and wisdom, and Karine's song beautifully captures these ideas and links them to the annual renewal of life and land each spring.

"My favourite place is in Angus. The Picts left lots of standing stones and there is one of these about two miles from where I live. From that place you get the most magnificent view of the southern Grampians spread out before you."

199

ANDY SCOTT

sculptor

A world-renowned sculptor, Andy's monumental works are to be found as far afield as Australia, although most are in the UK. His Heavy Horse on the M8 motorway between Glasgow and Edinburgh is seen by 100,000 people daily, and one of his most recent and celebrated works is The Kelpies in Falkirk. He also created the Ibrox disaster memorial statue featuring footballing legend John Greig at Rangers' stadium.

THE CITYSCAPE OF GLASGOW is my strongest inspiration. I was born in Springburn, brought up in Pollokshields, trained at the Glasgow School of Art and my studio is in Maryhill. I started really looking at the city from a very young age. My father was an architectural draughtsman and he used to take me around the streets and tell me to look up above the shop fronts and see the magnificent buildings. The Victorian architecture and the wonderful statuary in Glasgow, the city's whole heritage, have always worked a kind of magic on me and, even now, I look at it and think how beautiful it all is. So that's where my inspiration comes from – not from the rolling hills of the Trossachs, lovely as they are.

My parents weren't artists as such, but as a child I was surrounded by good art with prints on the walls at home, and they used to take us kids to the galleries at Kelvingrove to see the paintings and other works of art. I was always quite arty as a child, painting, scribbling and creating things with Lego – like most youngsters, I suppose. The difference was that I continued that interest and felt it was what I wanted to do with my life. It seemed I had some ability and my parents were very supportive – they never told me to pack it in and get a 'proper' job – so I was lucky on both counts.

I went to lunchtime classes at the Glasgow School of Art and a residential art course at Castle Toward and these were pivotal for me. You can only be taught so much at school, and once you've grasped the basics that's usually as far as school can take you. But going to these classes meant I could get my hands on new materials for the first time and really work out in which direction I

wanted to take things. It opened my eyes to a whole new world and I will always be grateful for it.

Having the aptitude and the determination to make art your job is one thing but having it all work out for you is another. Ten years after I left art school I was turning my hand to all sorts of things to make a living, then I won the commission to produce the *Heavy Horse*. That changed everything for me and I knew then that this is what I wanted to be doing. *Heavy Horse* is still probably my favourite work.

Given that *The Kelpies* came along later you might think I was some kind of horse expert, but I wasn't, although I found out that my great-grandfather used to work with horses. I used to go to the stables at the Pollok estate and use the horses there as my models. I became very good friends with the Clydesdale as a breed – the traditional working horse. After *Heavy Horse* was unveiled with quite a fanfare I thought the phone would be ringing non-stop. That didn't happen but commissions gradually started to come in.

I'm best known for my steel sculptures so that's the kind of work I spend most of my time doing – you become a willing victim of your own portfolio, in a way – but I also like to work with clay and bronze, so doing the statue of John Greig for Rangers to mark the Ibrox disaster was a privilege. My father was at the game in 1971 when it happened and 66 people lost their lives. He came through the match unscathed physically, but the disaster affected everyone emotionally. I remember even as a little kid what a huge effect it had, so it was a very humbling experience to create something that symbolised

such an emotive event. I think it's a very powerful piece and I couldn't have done it without the vital help of my colleague Alison Bell.

People often don't realise the number of people who are behind producing large sculptures, especially something the size of *The Kelpies* which are 30 metres tall and weigh 300 tonnes each. It was a project that was eight-and-a-half years in the making, from the first sketch to completion. Hundreds of people were involved in making it happen – I'm just the centre forward who scored the goal and got the plaudits, but there was a whole team involved. It was a huge part of my life and something that happens once in a lifetime. My father was from Falkirk, so I'm particularly pleased that it's had such a transformative effect on the town. Apart from having a huge number of visitors, it's a sculpture that local people have embraced and have developed a sense of ownership towards. It's all part of the Helix Park project which has a regeneration and environmental ethos and I'm honoured to have played a part in it.

You have to congratulate Falkirk Council and Scottish Canals for sticking to their guns. There were a lot of challenges during the whole process and it would have been easy to walk away but they had the tenacity to see it through. That's something that I think should happen more in Scotland. The people are fantastic but bureaucracy is a problem and too often good ideas fall by the wayside. I don't think we celebrate success enough. Modesty is a two-sided thing. It's an endearing quality but, if you're too hesitant about blowing your own trumpet, great ideas and creative opportunities can be lost.

Heavy Horse on the M8 motorway

My hero and role model in so many ways is Charles Rennie Mackintosh. At one point he was shunned by Glasgow and Scotland but he persevered and now his design skill is part of the fabric of the city. Without the Glasgow School of Art that he designed I wouldn't be where I am now. When it went up in flames in 2014 there was a sense of loss throughout the whole city, not just among art graduates. It was like hearing an old friend was mortally ill. But everyone has rallied round and everyone thinks it can and will be restored to its former glory.

Now I live in the West End of Glasgow. You walk around the Botanic Gardens and you could be in the middle of the country. It all blends in so well with the built environment. The whole thing becomes part of your very soul. I also like wandering round the south side of the city with its grand old mansions. It must have been the Scottish equivalent of Beverly Hills in Victorian times with its wealth and the grid network of the streets. In contrast, I love the Finnieston crane on the Clyde. It's a reminder of what Glasgow used to be – a busy, busy city whose purpose was to be a leading manufacturer of many things as well as ships. It embodies the indomitable spirit of the place and of Glaswegians themselves. No matter how much local authorities try to hide it, it's still there and it still stands proud.

scottssculptures.co.uk

"I love the Finnieston crane on the Clyde. It embodies the indomitable spirit of the place and of Glaswegians themselves. No matter how much local authorities try to hide it, it's still there and it still stands proud."

DOUGRAY SCOTT
actor

Following his early television appearance in Soldier Soldier, *Dougray made his mark in the film* Twin Town. *He went on to star in a raft of Hollywood movies including* Mission: Impossible ll *with Tom Cruise,* Enigma *alongside Kate Winslet and* Taken 3 *with Liam Neeson. He also had a regular role in the US television series* Desperate Housewives.

MY DAD WAS A SALESMAN, and watching him work had a big influence on me. In some ways it's a very similar job to acting and I think it's thanks to that experience that I became what I am. The other great part of his job was that he would travel all around Scotland and I'd often go with him. That's how I really got to know and love my country. We'd go north to south, east to west, right into the Highlands – everywhere.

It wasn't on the cards that I would become an actor, though. Where I was brought up in Glenrothes in Fife the jobs that were the most likely choices were at the Rosyth dockyards or other industries in the area. Otherwise it was joining the Army or maybe the Navy if you were lucky. None of that appealed to me. I knew from the age of 14 I wanted to be an actor but it was a very unusual ambition where I was from. There was no one else apart from me who wanted to do it and, at school, I was told in no uncertain terms that I'd never be an actor. But if someone tells me I can't do something I will try to prove I can.

We lived on the edge of a working-class area. There were a lot of factories around – in fact from our house we could see the Haig whisky factory which may or may not be attractive, depending on your point of view – but you could also see the Falkland Hills. There was a lot of fishing and mining in the area, but there was also a lot of farmland. It was a bit of a mixture. As a youngster a lot of my life was spent outdoors – climbing trees, playing football and tennis, and later golf, that kind of thing. Hibs was (and still is) my football team.

At school I loved English – that grabbed me very early on. I used to love reading plays, especially by Arthur Miller. I had a particular connection with his *Death of a Salesman* because of my father. I did a foundation course in drama in Kirkcaldy which was very good, then I went off to the Royal Welsh College of Music and Drama in Cardiff at the age of 18. I loved it. There were some people there who really encouraged me like the director Sue Dunderdale and I worked very hard. I was very studious – not at all your typical student.

I got a few parts, then being cast in *Twin Town* as a coked-out, psycho cop opened doors for me. One thing I'm really proud about is that I didn't let that stop me playing other kinds of parts. I wanted to play Prince Charming in *Ever After* but the director didn't think, after *Twin Town*, that I was right for it. I said of course I could be Prince Charming – I'm an actor, aren't I? And I got the role.

Bloody-mindedness is a typical Scottish trait – there is that steeliness, resolve, determination and grit in a lot of Scots. It's a cliché but it's true. You see it in so many people who've been a success in all walks of life.

As a kid and a Hibs fan, football played a huge part in my life, and my heroes were Pat Stanton and John Brownlie. In the showbusiness world, I admire Sean Connery and the film director Bill Douglas, and I think the writer Robin Jenkins who wrote *The Cone Gatherers* is phenomenal. I'm proud of being Scottish. It's what shaped me. I live in Los Angeles and London but Scotland is, and always will be, my spiritual home.

I often think of getting a place there and I would certainly move back if things worked out that way. Of course, there's not just me to take into consideration – I have a wife and kids – but it would be nice. I'm always

Dougray in his early acting days

*"The Trossachs are gorgeous.
I spent a lot of time there
when I was growing up."*

Rest and be Thankful: "It's unlike anywhere else on the planet."

surprised when Scottish people who've left home say they'd never go back. I feel most comfortable when I'm around Scottish people and I feel more comfortable in Scotland than anywhere else. It's my favourite country. Our countryside is the best in the world. I have never been anywhere that I think has better countryside. Our cities are pretty good too. I love Edinburgh. It's my favourite city and I think it's extraordinary.

My travels with my father were what gave me such a great early love of Scotland. My favourite place is the Mull of Kintyre – so good Paul McCartney wrote a song about it! It's a great journey from Glasgow to get there,

past Loch Fyne and down the peninsula with beautiful views of Gigha and Jura. I love it. I remember filming there when I did *The Crow Road*.

Then there's Sutherland in the north west, and the Black Isle and forest. And the Trossachs are gorgeous. I spent a lot of time there when I was growing up. There is a place when you drive out of Glasgow toward Kintyre called Rest and be Thankful. It's unlike anywhere else on the planet. Both of my parents are from Glasgow and when we had holidays it was always somewhere in Scotland in a caravan or a B&B. We never, ever had a Torremolinos type of family holiday.

As well as the places, there are also many songs that remind me of Scotland. I love *Caledonia* – it's maybe a little corny but it's nice. The Proclaimers' *Sunshine on Leith* is another – everyone at Hibs loves that one. Dick Gaughan's work is great, too. Probably the top of the list for me would be *Family Life* or *Saturday Night* by The Blue Nile. Those songs take me right back to a place where I feel incredibly happy.

"My favourite place is the Mull of Kintyre – so good Paul McCartney wrote a song about it! It's a great journey from Glasgow to get there, past Loch Fyne and down the peninsula with beautiful views of Gigha and Jura. I love it."

JOHN GORDON SINCLAIR
writer, actor

Renowned for starring in the 1981 film Gregory's Girl, *he also appeared in films as diverse as* Local Hero *in 1983 and* World War Z *with Brad Pitt in 2013. He has had numerous television roles and has also acted to much acclaim on stage, notably in* She Loves Me – *for which he received the Laurence Olivier Award – and* The Producers *in London's West End. He has written two novels:* Seventy Times Seven *and* Blood Whispers.

I DON'T THINK I'M AMBITIOUS. There was never any conscious decision in my mind that I would make films or perform on television and the stage as a job. I tend to be dragged through life by the hair. When I was young the convention was that you'd do what your dad did, and follow in his footsteps. My dad was an electrician, so the expectation was that I'd do the same and get a trade. University was never mentioned to me at my school and never presented as an option.

So I went to work for a firm called James Scott and did the first two years of my apprenticeship. I can still wire sockets and still have my original pair of pliers – so I've always got that to fall back on!

This was all happening at the same time as *Gregory's Girl*. The film was starting to take off but I don't think anyone had an idea of how successful it would be, but it opened up possibilities that I had to pursue. I talked to the firm to say I wanted to leave and they were very good about it – they said I didn't have to do the final year as I already had my qualifications. So off I went to London.

This was in September 1982 when I was 20. A few of my friends had moved there to go to art college, so I hooked up with the ex-pat gang. I didn't really have any English friends at the time. Having that Scottish background makes life a lot easier because Scots look out for each other – and they don't take themselves too seriously. We would rather laugh at ourselves than other people. My children were born in England, but they're not allowed to be too English! My wife is from Glasgow too, so they have Scottish blood. Nowadays I have one or two friends who are actors, and every now and then I quite enjoy the odd showbiz thing, but that's not how I

Dee Hepburn and John Gordon Sinclair in Gregory's Girl

"One of my favourite places is Whiteinch Park which is inside Glasgow's Victoria Park. There are lovely floral displays there and a boating pond."

see my life. My friends are still mostly the people I was at school with in Glasgow.

I was born in Partick and we moved to Scotstoun which was very close to the docks. I remember the sound of the horn going off at four o' clock in the morning calling the dock workers – I have haunting memories of that as a child.

When I think about my childhood I remember sunny days and long, hot summers. Considering it rains so much in Glasgow my brain must be playing tricks on me. I think I see things as a lot rosier than they probably were. I had a great time at primary school, but the first few years at secondary school were torturous. I wasn't that happy being around a load of delinquents and it could be a bit rough. When all the neds left school things got a lot better for me.

In years four and five I got a chance to flourish a bit more. The school had a strong English department and the teachers were very good. I'm still in contact with them and I thanked two of them – Isabelle McNaughton and Jim Mitchell – in the credits of my second novel *Blood Whispers*. They would take us to the theatre and gave us far more than just a basic education and I've always been grateful for that. They got me involved in the Glasgow Youth Theatre and that was where Bill Forsyth's early films like *That Sinking Feeling* and *Gregory's Girl* got started.

I have done a lot of different work in the acting world, and I tend to judge what I've done by the enjoyment factor. Doing *The Producers* on stage was professionally the best year I have ever had from that point of view. More recently it has been writing. Getting books published is great because it's something I've done myself – it's not someone else's writing or words.

If ever my books are made into films, I want the American pianist Mike Garson to play on them. I've already tweeted him about it! He played on David Bowie's *Aladdin Sane* which I used to listen to all the time when I was young. Bowie was this extraordinary creature and

John Gordon Sinclair in Local Hero *in 1983*

I had never seen anything like him in my life. Subliminally it had an impact on my life because he showed that anything is possible. When I listen to that it takes me right back to that time of my life as a Glasgow schoolboy.

The city itself and where I grew up in Partick and Scotstoun hold a lot of memories for me, and we often go back to visit as a family. My wife has relatives in Glasgow and I have an aunt in Partick and cousins in the area so I like to drive around there. We are never away from Glasgow long enough to miss it. One of my favourite places is Whiteinch Park which is inside Glasgow's Victoria Park. There are lovely floral displays there and a boating pond.

The place we try to go to whenever we can is Kippford on the Solway coast which is on about the same level as Carlisle. It's unspoilt and magical. When I go there I just want to sit down and never leave. I get that feeling every time I go there. I referenced Kippford in my second book, calling it Sceur. The scenery round the Urr estuary is spectacular. You can wander down forest tracks and, when the tide's out, walk across to Rough Island. It's utterly beautiful.

When Bill Forsyth was making *Local Hero* he was looking for a village on the coast that had one road and a forest track. He couldn't find it, so he filmed at two separate places and joined them together. He told me if he'd known about Kippford he'd have filmed there – he said he had dreamed of a place like that for the film. But it's one of those special places that you almost want to keep a secret. You don't want hordes of people going there.

"*Kippford on the Solway coast is unspoilt and magical.
When I go there I just want to sit down and never leave.*"

SIR JACKIE STEWART

racing driver

Known as the Flying Scotsman, Sir Jackie raced in Formula One competitions from 1965-1973, winning three World Drivers Championships. He was BBC Sports Personality of the Year in 1973, and in 2009 was voted fifth out of 50 top Formula One drivers. With his son Paul, he was principal of the Stewart Grand Prix Formula One racing team.

I BECAME A RACING DRIVER by accident when I was working as a mechanic. It certainly wasn't something I thought about as a child growing up in Milton near Dumbarton – or Dumbuck as we called it. I had a Hornby train set I used to play with, but there were no model racing cars. I was actually born at home in our house called Rockview. It's still there and now it has a blue plaque.

Outside of school, I had a normal childhood playing with my friends in the wide open spaces behind our house. There were two hills – Dumbuck Hill and Camelback – which were within walking distance and we'd spend a lot of time around there. School itself was a nightmare for me. I had undiagnosed dyslexia so I couldn't read and write correctly and just felt like a failure. Playing football was the only relief. I played for the school and the county but I couldn't get out of school quickly enough and I left as soon as I could at the age of 15.

One of my grandfathers was a gamekeeper and the other was a farmer so I grew up around typical Scottish countryside pursuits like shooting and fishing – and also deer-stalking on the bonnie, bonnie banks of Loch Lomond. Country living was a big part of my life and I learned about all the different activities from real experts. I would go salmon-fishing with my father on the Spey and around Aberlour. My father was a good fisherman and a good shot so I got into both sports. By the age of 15 I was working in my father's garage as a mechanic and I started to shoot competitively. The shooting really took off and I became part of the Scottish and Great Britain teams. It was a big adventure and suddenly my so-called childhood disappeared!

"I grew up around typical Scottish countryside pursuits like shooting and fishing – and deer-stalking on the bonnie, bonnie banks of Loch Lomond."

Motor racing came into my life initially because my brother Jim drove for Jaguar and was quite well known. I used to go to race meetings with him and I'd get the racers' autographs. I had an autograph book at the age of ten and I still treasure it today. When I started to work as a mechanic there were a lot of folk around with fancy cars who would bring them to us to take care of them because we were good at it. There was a young man who had some great cars but he wasn't allowed to drive them because of a clause in his family trust. Other people were allowed to drive the cars, though.

So I used to prepare those cars for races and I'd go to meetings and carry helmets, drive the cars to the starting line, that sort of thing. One day as a reward I was given the chance to try racing one of the cars – a Porsche – at Heathfield in Ayrshire. I came second and the next time I raced I won. So I was becoming more interested in racing, and around this time I gave up shooting and got married. Marriage can be an expensive business and I couldn't afford both. My story goes that I became a three-time world champion so I could afford the wife!

A lot of Scots are winners because they have a huge drive to succeed and to prove they're better than anyone else. I certainly hated being beaten. There's a bit of a chip on our shoulders. Whether you're talking about accountants, lawyers, engineers, businessmen – or racing drivers for that matter – there's that inbuilt ambition and desire to prove yourself. All the way from school right through life if you fail at something you feel you have your tail between your legs and that's a feeling you want to dispel. Even now I try as hard as I can to keep delivering for the people I work for. It's nothing to do with money – it's to do with doing a good job. I've been with Rolex, Moet & Chandon and Ford for over 40 years which I think tells its own story.

We can be a dour lot, we Scots. It takes a lot to win our trust but we do make a go of whatever life has to offer us. I like to think that, even with people who go on to succeed, we keep our feet on the ground. Take someone like Sean Connery. I got to know him in 1971 and I was really impressed by him. He's a globally famous man who still has a great deal of modesty about him. He doesn't feel the need to put on a show. Another Scot I admire is Sir William Purves, one of the greatest bankers of the 1990s, who made HSBC what it is today. From my younger years I looked up to the motorcyclist Bob McIntyre who was a fantastic racer but was very down-to-earth, had great attention to detail and was full of determination. Sadly he was killed in an accident at Oulton Park in1962.

There is obviously danger as well as glory in the racing world and it does take courage. I'm probably proudest of winning my first Grand Prix, my first World Championship and actually winning my last World Championship knowing I was never going to do it again. In my personal life I've enjoyed seeing my two sons and my grandchildren growing up happily and successfully.

My sons don't live in Scotland but, like me, they are proud Scots who love to go back to their homeland.

The three of us recently went on a journey to the north of Scotland. We based ourselves in Inverness but I thought they should see John O'Groats as they'd never been there before. The road journey there was nothing particularly special, but driving across the top of Scotland was just spectacular. We were in a Range Rover so we were high up and could see everything. What views! When I was little we didn't have long holidays as such. The garage was a family concern so my father would stay to look after it and my mother would take me off on short trips and often day trips down the coast of Ayrshire.

Music was another part of my childhood. As well as being active in the bowling club and the salmon club, my father was also in the Dumbarton Opera Society and he played the violin. If there's a tune that reminds me of Scotland it's the hymn *St Clement*. It's a lament, really, and I think it has a magnificently Scottish feel.

215

JANETTE TOUGH

performer

Best known as Wee Jimmy Krankie, Janette has worked in partnership with her husband Ian as The Krankies since the 1970s, with their famous catchphrase Fan-Dabi-Dozi. They performed in the Royal Variety Show in 1978, made numerous appearances on Crackerjack, had their own TV shows including The Krankies Club and have featured in French and Saunders. They have been a mainstay of pantomime for many years.

I WAS AN OFFICE JUNIOR in Reliance Telephones in Glasgow at the age of 16 when fate came knocking. It came about because one of my colleagues, Ron Robson, was amused that I used steps to do the filing because I was so little. We got talking and he told me that his wife was in showbusiness and that he had also been in that world himself some years back. He asked me if I'd ever considered a career in showbusiness. I hadn't really, but he saw something in me – some kind of character and comedy potential – and he took me to an audition at the Gaiety Theatre in Ayr. I sang *Baby Face* – and immediately got a part in panto.

Some things are just meant to be. If I hadn't been working in that office at that time I don't think I'd be where I am today.

Like lots of other kids, though, I used to like to sing and dance. I went to dance classes when I was seven where I learned tap and ballet and I would sing in concerts, but I don't think I stood out in terms of talent or anything – I was just a schoolchild like the rest.

I went to Chapel Green primary school in a little village called Queenzietown near Kilsyth where I was brought up. It was a wee place with one shop and there wasn't much going on. Our entertainment was playing on the swings or running around in the hills. It was nice and friendly, but sometimes it would drive you mad as a youngster wanting to be in the middle of things.

My dad was a mining engineer and had an Austin car. Every Sunday we'd drive out to see my gran and grandpa, and sometimes we would take trips further away to Stonehaven and St Andrews. The big thing for me in those days was being a Girl Guide. I was a first class guide, a patrol leader, which meant I could take the guides camping to Leckie near Stirling and I would get to sleep at the front of the tent.

My world changed when I got that panto role. It was at the Pavilion Theatre in Glasgow. I was working with the comic Jack Milroy who was playing Widow Cranky and I was playing one of his six children. At the time I was 16 but I probably only looked about nine. Jack was brilliant. He took me under his wing, taught me facial expressions and moulded me into playing comedy. If I made a mistake like tripping over my nightdress and he thought it was funny he'd say: "Keep that one in for the next show!"

I'd never been to the theatre before – the first panto I saw was the one I was in – but it has played a big part of my life since then. Ian and I have had a smashing time in the last few years performing in panto in Glasgow with John Barrowman and we've become good friends.

Although Ian and I divide our time now between our homes in Torquay and Australia, it's always great to come home. I find Scotland the easiest place to work for laughs. It's great to use your own accent and not have to think too much about whether people will understand what you are going to say – everyone 'gets' you and it's so relaxing and natural.

But in fact, I've only spent a fraction of my working life in Scotland. After three years working at the Pavilion I teamed up with one of the other girls, Margaret Murray, and we set off for the cabaret rooms in the clubs in Manchester. We found ourselves working alongside blue

Janette with her early stage partner Margaret Murray

comics and strippers and it was quite an eye-opener. I remember one of the strippers asking to borrow my lipstick, then she lifted up her jumper and painted her nipples with it. I don't think I asked for it back! It wasn't necessarily what we were expecting but it was a good, tough training ground.

Later I went back to Glasgow and met Ian. We got together as a couple and also started working together. I was Little Jimmy Krankie and he was the father figure. We went back to the clubs and also played summer seasons around the UK. I remember the South Pier in Blackpool being on the same bill as Freddie and the Dreamers, Susan Maughan, Ivor Emmanuel from Wales and the Irish comic Mike Newman. We were the Scottish act, and on the bill our stage name 'The Krankies' was dwarfed by the words 'From Scotland'. We worked abroad too in Germany, Italy and Turkey and even played to American soldiers going out to Vietnam.

Our biggest success in those years was being in the Royal Variety Show in 1978. We really felt we'd 'arrived' and it was a very proud moment for us.

It's funny that we're so well known primarily for being Scottish – I'm not sure why that is, but I'm not complaining. There has been a lot of attention on Scotland recently and it's good to see my home country being in the spotlight.

Glasgow is the city I love most. It's great to go out and find so many places where you can eat, drink and just walk around. The way that the banks of the Clyde have completely transformed is astonishing. It's such a hive of activity for entertainment. I especially love it at night, when you see the theatres and concert halls and the SECC complex all lit up. I especially love the Clyde Auditorium which is known as the Armadillo – our own Sydney Opera House. It's so beautiful. And if I had to pick my favourite place of all it would be Buchanan Street. It was always buzzing in the past, and it still is.

krankies.com

Janette and Ian: The Krankies

MIDGE URE OBE

musician

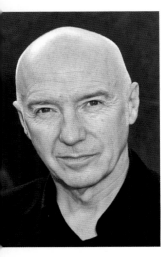

Midge enjoyed early chart success in the 1970s and 1980s in bands including Slik, Rich Kids, Visage and as frontman of Ultravox. In 1984 he co-wrote and produced the Band Aid charity single Do They Know It's Christmas? *which has sold 3.7million copies and is the second highest selling single in UK chart history. He co-organised Live Aid with Bob Geldof the following year. Still touring and recording, he serves as an ambassador for Save the Children.*

THERE ARE TWO PIECES OF MUSIC that always remind me of Scotland. One of the most haunting, lamenting beautiful pieces of music is the *Bonnie Black Isle*. I played that at my father's funeral. It has a lovely sad, distant melody. It's probably where I get my sense of musical drama. The other is Rabbie Burns' *A Red, Red Rose* because I won an award for singing that when I was in primary school. That was my first pat on the back and it could so easily have been my last.

It's very difficult to say what my proudest moment is. People talk about Band Aid and it was phenomenal to perform *Vienna* at Live Aid to 1.9 billion people worldwide. I've even got five honorary degrees which is amazing for someone who could never get anywhere near a university. But – whether it's the Queen pinning on your OBE or getting an Ivor Novello Award – any sort of recognition that proves that Victorianesque school-teacher wrong is good. The one who thought you were a useless brat and told you in no uncertain terms that you would never amount to anything. Any kind of acclaim that proves the old battleaxe wrong is a good thing.

I occasionally play a gig at the old Renfrew Ferry in Glasgow, which has become a little music venue. And there's a little glass wall with dates running through history featuring all the names of great Scots who have changed people's lives – people like John Logie Baird and Charles Rennie Mackintosh – and I'm on there somewhere. It's totally humbling seeing my name next to theirs.

Mackintosh was brilliant. I feel a slight empathy with him trying to be artistic in a world that didn't want artistic people. It must have been so much more difficult for him to be so radical in dark, gloomy Victorian times. He was a beam of sunshine trying to create beautiful buildings.

> ## " To a kid growing up it was like a big playground – a Glasgow Disneyland

I went to the same primary school in Cambuslang – which is three miles outside Glasgow – as my mother. In fact the janitor who was there when she was at school was still there when I attended in the late 1950s. The building is still there but it's an old people's home now so I could end up going back! Those were the days when you would get the strap just for talking in class. School meant humiliation and abuse. But I didn't know any better: it was just what life was.

It was the same growing up in the one-bedroom tenement block we called home. There was a kitchenette with a cavity bed (I think they are peculiar to Glasgow) – basically a cupboard in a wall with a mattress, which is where my parents slept. There was a sitting room with a sink and a cooker in a tiny hallway and a bedroom where I slept with my brother. There was the stagnant water in what was laughingly known as the backyard. There were outside toilets and washhouses, stinking drains and trashed cars so it looked like a bomb site. But you didn't know any better. It was the same for everyone.

Midge performing Vienna *with Ultravox at Live Aid 1985*

You would only know it was bad if you had something to gauge it by. And to a kid growing up it was like a big playground – a Glasgow Disneyland.

Then I went to Rutherglen Academy because my older brother went there. That was the posh grammar school but I only got in because I had a high IQ. I wasn't particularly good at anything apart from painting and music. But they didn't want to teach me music and art, and in those days if you weren't heading for university you were factory fodder.

"When I get up past Fort William and the Kyle of Lochalsh and Plockton – where they filmed the TV show Hamish Macbeth *– the countryside is simply stunning and I get a distinct feeling of déjà vu."*
Plockton

I hated it, so I left school at 15 and went to technical college for six months because I was too young to start an apprenticeship. That was already a massive step up from my dad who was a van driver. It was seen as a good thing to be a skilled worker. It was a job for life if that's what you wanted – unlike today when there are no jobs for life. Out of 500 kids I got one of ten apprenticeships to work at the National Engineering Laboratories in East Kilbride but I left after six months to pursue music.

The music was always there since I was ten. My parents bought me a great old dance band guitar, which was 40 years old then, and I still have it to this day. So I taught myself music and I could always sing – that was free. I've no idea where the music came from. My grandmother had a piano and my dad played it off-key like Les Dawson, except he didn't mean to. We'd bang out *Can You Wash a Sailor's Shirt* and drive everybody crazy. The radio was on all the time and I heard everything from Frank Sinatra to The Beatles. Melody was a big thing in the early 1960s and everything I do is very melodic. I can still hear bits of old songs – like *Johnny Remember Me* and the old traditional Scottish music you were fed at school – in my work.

We didn't have a family car so summer holidays would be out to the Clyde and Ayrshire coast. We'd borrow a car from one of my dad's brothers and visit old Victorian seaside places like Ayr and Largs. Those days still hold great memories even though a holiday was going somewhere not as nice as home. We didn't have any money so it was an ice-cream and a walk along the promenade. We would rent a little flat which was invariably worse than the damp, cold and miserable one we left at home and we'd cook on an old Victorian fire. I remember being in that flat in August 1962 when the news broke that Marilyn Monroe was dead, my parents going on about it and not understanding what the big fuss was all about.

In a previous life I must have come from the Islands and Highlands. For someone who was brought up in

deepest, darkest Glasgow I get a feeling of immense wellbeing when I'm there. When I get up past Fort William and the Kyle of Lochalsh and Plockton – where they filmed the TV show *Hamish Macbeth* – the countryside is simply stunning and I get a distinct feeling of déjà vu. Mull is one of my favourite places because it's so diverse. You have the glorious white sand and aquamarine clear water of the Gulf Stream and behind you 900-feet-high cliffs.

I used to go up there for holidays when the kids were young. I remember renting this little cottage on the island of Mull and standing on the road next to it was this magnificent stag. A marketing man's dream! It must be one of the few places in the UK where you can escape and be completely on your own, at one with nature. There's nothing manufactured or manipulated about it. Sheer beauty.

We live in Bath now and the quality of life is superb but I'd move back to Scotland in a heartbeat. It's not just my decision because the kids are grown up now and

their sights are set further afield. But I totally get it. From Glasgow within half an hour in any direction you can be in the most stunning countryside imaginable. Back in the 1980s you had to be in London if you were in the music industry but that's not the case any more with the internet and mobile phones.

But for me it's the people of Scotland that are special and make it such an exceptional place, from the dour Scot in TV's *Dad's Army* to the nicest, funniest people you could ever wish to meet. The Scots have put up with an awful lot of crap for hundreds of years but there's a great sense of humour, a warmth and resilience and a wonderful attitude towards life.

midgeure.com

"Mull is one of my favourite places because it's so diverse. You have the glorious white sand and aquamarine clear water of the Gulf Stream and behind you 900-feet-high cliffs."
Sunset view from Kintra on the Ross of Mull

JACK VETTRIANO OBE
artist

Scotland's most celebrated artist, Jack has an instantly recognisable style that has caught the eye of collectors including Sir Alex Ferguson, Sir Terence Conran and Jack Nicholson. His painting The Singing Butler has been Britain's best-selling image. Awarded the OBE in 2003, he went on to win the Great Scot of the Year award in 2010.

THE COAST AT LEVEN is where I got the ideas for the beach scenes in my paintings. There is a very, very long beach of pure, clean sand before you hit the water. You can walk a hundred yards and your feet are still dry. It's very beautiful.

As a kid, though, painting was the last thing on my mind. I grew up in Methil, Fife which is next to Leven. At that time coal was king and my family lived in what we call a miners' row – a terrace of one-storey houses. I had an absolutely marvellous childhood, running around with my friends, going to the woods, collecting birds' eggs, gathering chestnuts. Each season had its speciality. We had a wonderful time and it never occurred to us that anything bad could happen.

But I didn't like school. I just couldn't be bothered with it. When I went to secondary school I wanted to leave as soon as I could. I was keen to get a job and earn enough money to buy a car. I really wanted to be a teddy boy but I was too late for that era so I started to dress like James Bond in a dark suit and straight, black, knitted tie. I didn't see anything unusual in that, but the way I dressed was certainly unusual in my house.

I managed to get a trade as an engineer with the Coal Board and I saved up to buy a car, as I planned. I was more interested in the opposite sex than in standing in a pub playing darts or dominoes. A lot of people were heavily into pub culture, and jeans and a Scotland football jersey were the standard uniform. Not for me. In my eyes I was James Bond and I really enjoyed those wonderful teen years of discovery.

It wasn't until I was in my early twenties that I started painting. I'd done the odd bit of sketching before that but

that was all. A girl I was going out with at the time gave me a box of paints – watercolours – for my birthday. In amongst the cards and the chocolate oranges there was this box of paints and I thought I'd see what this was all about. I was very into classic cars and I would get pictures of cars and copy them. I enjoyed it, and I started to paint more and more but I never thought it was going anywhere. It was just a hobby.

Then I got a job in the Middle East and I was painting all the time out there. I could see that something was happening. At the time I had a girlfriend in Scotland, so I came back home and got married. I spent most of my time doing up houses, buying and selling, just trying to improve our lot. At one point we had a house with an extra room so I bought an easel and started to paint a lot more. I could see fairly quickly that I had a gift.

The problem with amateur artists is that often they don't use their imagination or they're frightened of what their imagination is. They don't want to try anything new or different in case people ask: "What the hell is that?" I suppose at that stage I was a bit like that, so I would go to the library and get a book on painting and, by copying what I saw, I learned my craft. If you throw in all those artists I admired like Monet, Manet, Van Gogh and Caravaggio then add me you have got my style of painting.

I'm proud I have my own style and I'm grateful for that. People know my paintings from a distance and that is quite rare. Sometimes I go to exhibitions and I see people are now copying me.

I finally became a full-time painter in 1989. I lived in Edinburgh and managed to live in some fabulous houses

The Missing Man

"The coast at Leven is where I got the ideas for the beach scenes in my paintings. There is a very, very long beach of pure, clean sand before you hit the water. It's very beautiful."

Long Time Gone

which became the backdrop to a lot of my paintings. Edinburgh is lovely but it's not a big place. I was beginning to get quite well known and I needed a change. I went to London for an exhibition and it was one of those situations where you go on holiday for a week and never come back. I lived for a while near Harrods and there were always lots of beautiful people around there. If there's one thing I love it's my visual senses being pleased. I love to look at lovely things, whether it's a car, a stiletto heel or a woman.

But I never left Scotland behind completely. Until recently I had a studio in Kirkcaldy and now I have a studio in Edinburgh as well as London. I also have a little apartment in Nice and a townhouse in Edinburgh. I usually fly back to Scotland and I love the view from the aeroplane as you're getting close to Edinburgh Airport. The flightpath cuts across the Forth towards Fife and then takes a sharp left. When I see Fife I always get a tingle. That coastline tells me I'm home. Just throw in a song by the master – Robbie Burns – such as *A Red, Red Rose* or *A Fond Kiss* and that is Scotland for me.

The painting of mine that I think is one of my most Scottish works is *Long Time Gone*. It's a scene which now no longer exists of a couple kissing in front of a huge power station between Leven and Methil which has been pulled down.

The one person I really have to thank for getting me on the path to success is a journalist called W. Gordon Smith. He was the art critic on Scotland on Sunday. He had heard of me and came to the studio to see my work. He said: "My God – where the hell have you been?" and he really encouraged me. He said I should paint whatever it was that did it for me: I should plough my own furrow. Also, I didn't realise how the world of galleries and commissions worked and he helped me along the way, becoming almost like a father figure. I'll never forget him.

Affirmation from people you respect is always a nice thing. Francis Bacon is my idol and he said my work was very well done. He said it may not have been his particular style and was a bit commercial for him, but nevertheless he said I was a good painter. A number of well-known people like Jack Nicholson, Sir Alex Ferguson, Robbie Coltrane, Tim Rice and Sir Terence Conran have bought my paintings and gone on record to support me. You'd be mad not to be pleased that people like that admire your work.

But the establishment in Edinburgh has not been so receptive. My first exhibition was panned and I'm afraid my impact in Edinburgh was nil. In Edinburgh you really have to die before they notice you. Glasgow is different. In Glasgow they seem much more able to accept young and living artists. The Glasgow Museum at Kelvingrove recently held a retrospective of my work and it broke all records, with 130,000 people visiting the exhibition. That surely tells its own story. I think there is room for both ground-breaking work and also art that the public actually wants to see.

jackvettriano.com

*"I love the view from the aeroplane as you're getting
close to Edinburgh Airport. The flightpath cuts across the
Forth towards Fife and then takes a sharp left. When I
see Fife I always get a tingle, knowing that I'm home."*

227

SHEENA WELLINGTON

folk singer

A traditional Scottish singer, Sheena performed at the opening ceremony of the Scottish Parliament in 1999. She has toured extensively at home and abroad and has recorded internationally-acclaimed albums. A highly influential advocate of her craft, she was installed in the Scottish Traditional Music Hall of Fame in 2009.

SINGING AT THE OPENING of the Scottish Parliament in 1999 was my proudest moment professionally. You couldn't top that. It was incredible to be asked. The existence of a Scottish Parliament is important to me and it was something my father had dreamed of for years.

I was asked to sing Robert Burns' *A Man's a Man for a' That*, which was an inspired choice for the occasion. It was decided, apparently, that to have a woman singing it would signal the inclusive Scotland we wanted to see. It's a fabulous international song of humanity and I will resist any attempt to hijack it as our national anthem. It was certainly a great moment for me, but I'm still slightly surprised, and a little humbled, when people come up and talk to me about it.

It's funny with major occasions like that how smooth it all looks from the outside. We had a hilarious time getting into the building. The current Scottish Parliament had yet to be built and the opening was in its temporary home in the General Assembly Hall of the Church of Scotland on the Mound. It's no great distance from Waverley but we kept being stopped to let the car bringing the Scottish Crown – and the Duke of Hamilton – sweep past. At the hall we were directed to the wrong room where I found the entire Inverness Gaelic Choir getting into their kilts. I eventually got the right room but as it was the only one with a mirror and washbasin the women from the choir were popping in and out. They are lovely people so that wasn't a problem and their company helped calm the nerves!

It seems a world away from my childhood in Dundee. I think of myself as a Lochee lass. Lochee was

Sally Magnusson, a piper, actress Lynn Ferguson, Sheena, Donald Dewar MP and writer Ruth Wishart

a distinct village until the early part of the 20th century, but though it has been a district of the city for almost 100 years, in my childhood we still spoke of going 'into Dundee'. It had what was at one time the largest textile factory in the world which boasted a spectacular Italianate chimney stack. The stack is still there – and it is still looking ornamental.

It was a close community and you knew who everyone was. Unfortunately, that meant everyone knew who you were so you couldn't get away with anything as a child! But we had a lot of freedom to roam around. There weren't many cars in those days and there were even some carts still being pulled by Clydesdale horses. We kids were always outside. You would just grab an old

"The existence of a Scottish Parliament is important to me and it was something my father had dreamed of for years."

haversack and maybe somebody's old gas mask holder (because it was just after the war), a bottle of water and a couple of pieces of bread and jam. There'd be four or six of you and nobody worried about you when you disappeared all day, only coming back at tea-time.

Even in the centre of Dundee it was the same. I lived for a while with my granny in the Hawkhill area. You still felt you were protected. There were always people about on the street getting their messages – shopping – and in the evening the men would be standing outside leaning against the wall and having a chat. Television hadn't come on the scene at that time. Mothers and grannies would be leaning on their window sills and everybody kept an eye on you. Sometimes I resented it a bit because you'd be climbing up something and be told to get off. And if news of what you had been up to got back to the house before you did you'd get spanked!

Looking back it seems like another world. When I was a teenager you'd go to things like 'ban the bomb' demos but it was always very respectable. The men would be in overcoats and the women in their Sunday best clothes. Hardly any women would have dreamed of wearing trousers in those days.

From as far back as I can remember I was always singing – my family were musical and my father and grandmother sang around the house –and people used to say to my family: "You should do something with that lassie's voice." I used to think it would be nice to be a singer but I didn't know how to go about it. There were plenty of clubs but I was quite shy so I didn't really push it.

I was actually planning to be a teacher but I had my appendix out, with complications, and missed a lot of my course. My health wasn't the best at the time, but it was essential that I got a proper job so I joined the WRNS as I always fancied the sea. I met my husband Malcolm when I was stationed in Lossiemouth, and we lived for a number of years in Somerset, Fife and Southampton before we went to St Andrews to run a guesthouse.

At that point singing wasn't really a big part of my life, and my career got started more or less by accident. We were next door to a folk club and, although I didn't have time to go during the holiday season, I wandered round when things were quieter. There was a ceilidh going on. I asked the compère if I could sing something and he said: "Oh aye! Maybe! We have a lot of singers here, you know." But he put me on at ten past 11, I got to do an encore and then I was asked to be a resident singer.

After that I sang at the club and folk festivals and things just snowballed. I was asked to do a folk programme on Radio Tay for a six-week trial. It wasn't until eight years later that I left the building.

Around that time the piper Hamish Moore moved into a house opposite and he was friends with Dougie MacLean, who wrote *Caledonia*. We all got friendly and we went to a wee party at Hamish's house where there was lots of singing. Dougie was, let's say, 'well-refreshed', but he declared: "I have to record you" and he invited me to his studio in Dunkeld.

I don't know what I was expecting but it was not state-of-the-art. In fact in those days it was almost like a Heath Robinson drawing, in contrast to today's Butterstone studios which would be envied by NASA! Some of the electricity wires were tied up with bits of tinfoil and if you wanted an echo effect you had go into the bathroom. It was freezing because you couldn't have the heating on at the same time as you were recording because of the background hum – Dougie MacLean has bat-like hearing. Still, thanks to Dougie's skill, I managed to record my first album, which came out to amazing reviews, and I later toured with Dougie a couple of times. There were American tours and various festivals and I sort of became established.

I'm sure being Scots had a lot to do with my being able to make it as a singer. There is a tradition of singing in the house and at parties and there were lots of good songs about. Despite the best efforts of school, I'm not from the 'hands clasped below the bosom' school of

singing, but traditional music was all around. I sing still for the love of the songs. I've never been that ambitious for myself so I sometimes feel quite surprised to find myself performing on a large stage in a large hall.

I'm told my mother was a good singer but she died when I was little more than a baby and sadly I don't remember her. But there have been plenty of people I've taken inspiration from down the years. Apart from my family, there are a lot of fine Scottish singers like the late Ray Fisher. She had what I call a proper folk voice, one that you could sharpen an axe with. I also really admired Jean Redpath. She blazed a trail in America like Alex Campbell did in Europe.

For me, though I've enjoyed the trips to the US, the Far East and Europe, the tours and the big gigs, Scotland is always where I've wanted to be. Being back in Dundee now seems right – we've come home to roost. My husband was brought up in Hampshire but Scotland is home to him, too. It's hard to get him south of the border these days!

There's something about Dundee and the surrounding area that has always drawn me back. It's a beautiful city – although various corporations down the years have done their level best to destroy it. In Dundee itself you've got all the amenities like theatres, museums, galleries, shops and restaurants but there's also a lovely harbour, and the hills and the beaches are only ten minutes away. We have some wonderful views. You go to the top of Dundee Law, the higher of the two hills which rise in the heart of the city, and you can see for miles out to sea and to the distant hills of Perthshire, Fife and Angus. It's utterly stunning.

sheena-wellington.co.uk

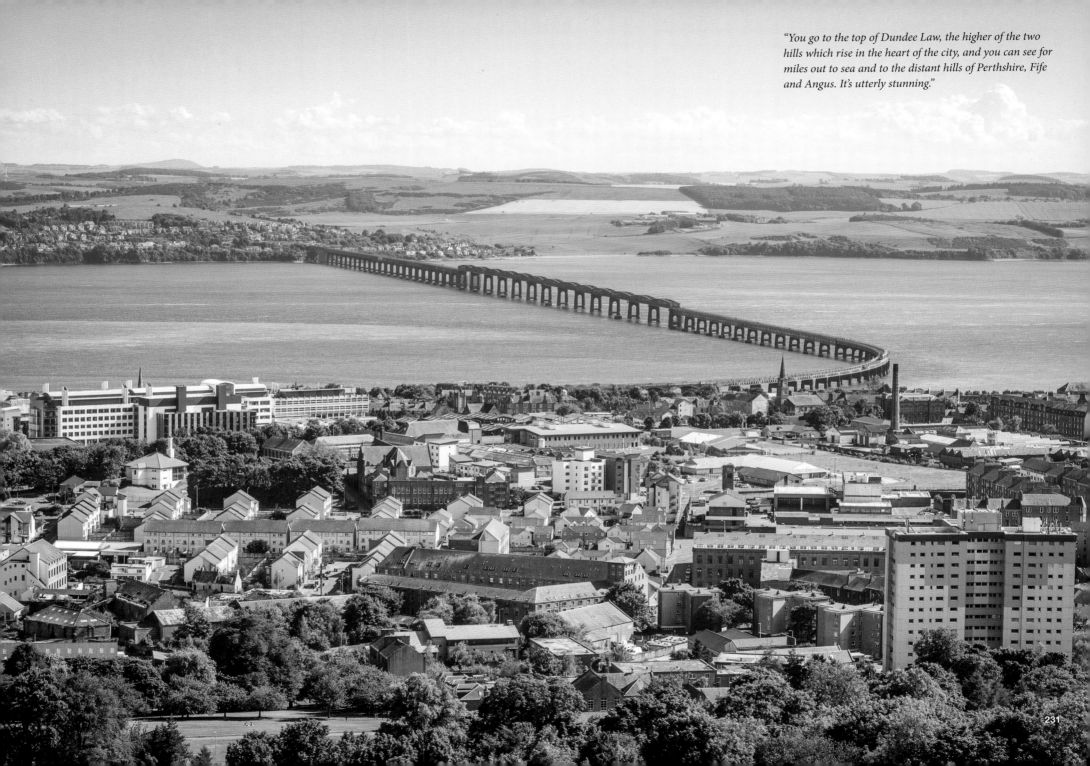

"You go to the top of Dundee Law, the higher of the two hills which rise in the heart of the city, and you can see for miles out to sea and to the distant hills of Perthshire, Fife and Angus. It's utterly stunning."

IRVINE WELSH
writer

Writer of novels, stories, plays and screenplays, Irvine shot to fame with his first novel Trainspotting *in 1993. It was later made into an award-wining film. In his words, he has never had to get a proper job since. His latest work,* A Decent Ride, *is equally controversial and also revolves around the grittier side of life in Edinburgh.*

I WAS ALWAYS A COMPULSIVE READER. When I was at primary school I used to love the Willard Price books about two brothers who went to explore the world looking for wild animals and having adventures. When I went to secondary school I got into skinhead books by Richard Allen – who is actually Canadian –about a skinhead called Joe Hawkins who later became a suedehead. They were all about adolescent sex and violence and I thought they were fantastically cool. A lot of the other books I was interested in were about travel and different countries. I always wanted to travel. And maps – I loved them.

I didn't spend all my time around books, though. I loved playing football and I liked going to the boxing club. I grew up in Leith and later Muirhouse. In Muirhouse the library was somewhere you only went when it was cold. The rest of the time we'd be out kicking the ball around. Everybody from the council schemes would play and you'd have games that went on for so long you forgot the score. It was a weird test of endurance.

I always liked both sport and art. You feel you are pushed into choosing between the two very early, but I didn't. I had two sets of friends – the wilder, crazier kids and the swots.

My first words were "Willie Bauld", the name of the legendary Hearts player. My dad and uncle used to compete with each other to see who could get me to say my first words – they had to be either "Willie Bauld" or "Gordon Smith" (who played mainly for Hibs but also later for Hearts). When I first started going to football matches it was mainly to Hearts as a family day out. Later, when I began to go with my mates instead, we'd go

to Hibs and I became a hard-core Hibs fan. My heroes were Pat Stanton, Peter Cormack, Colin Stein and Peter Marinello. We had a good Hibs team then, for five or six years. I thought it was going to be like that all the time – challenging for cups and titles and getting into Europe – but it was an aberration.

I was also massively into glam rock. I liked bands like T Rex but David Bowie was the one who really stood out. As far as I was concerned, Bowie was the key. He was such a charismatic character with an eclectic musical background and he as good as educated a whole generation. When he came out of the glam thing he went on to other things and that got us into Iggy Pop, Lou Reed, the Velvet Underground, soul, electronic music. As a kind of working-class artist he was a role model. He made you feel that, even if life seemed to be constraining you, you could change your persona and be what you wanted.

I was also obsessed by films from an early stage. I'd go to the Salon cinema in Edinburgh and watch cartoons. At cinemas you'd usually get two features and you could be there all day. It was a bit like going to football games: you'd get into it and become obsessed. I remember when *Enter the Dragon* with Bruce Lee came out and we'd come out of the cinema doing kung fu kicks.

I only dabbled in writing a little bit. I didn't think it was a serious thing. I wasn't from that background of culture with a drawing room full of books. Books were more of a communal thing that you'd pass around. Your mum would get something from your auntie or your dad would get a book from your uncle and maybe you would get to read it too. There was no room in our house

for bookshelves or a desk where you could sit down and write.

I didn't conceptualise myself as a writer – it took a while for that to happen. I had been doing it for years before it sunk in that there was a reason why I was writing all the time. Once you give it a kind of respect you start to see yourself in that way and that's what you become. It's an epiphany, really.

When *Trainspotting* came out I thought it was original and strong and that it had a voice, but there have been a lot of good books down the years so I didn't have particularly high expectations. But it got quite a lot of attention and I thought it would maybe do OK in Edinburgh amongst the cognoscenti. I didn't expect it to have the success it did. For me, it was my calling card rather than an albatross round my neck. And thanks to *Trainspotting* I've never had to get a proper job since.

If you're writing about difficult things like violence and addiction, comedy is a way of getting you to engage with them. Black humour can make painful things easier, I think. If you are a writer and you present your reader with that kind of material, you have a responsibility to get it across. People need a bit of space and, if you set it up in a comedic way, it doesn't seem so scary or horrible and humour gives you that space. If you look at that kind of stuff on screen you are a prisoner of the director's vision. In a book you are dealing with it in your head, so you can add all the bunnies and kittens and puppies if you need to. Life is beautiful but it's also ridiculous and you can't take it too seriously.

In my books I like to write in the way people in Edinburgh speak. It's not that big an idea. I admired it in

"I love the view of the castle when you get out of the station and look up at it. The best view is from Princes Street or Alfred Steet. It's best admired from a distance."

other writers' work and it seemed to be more real, more accurate. When I first started to write I wrote speech in regular English and it just seemed so flat and pretentious and dull. My characters don't speak like that. To find their spirit I had to go back to the vernacular. It's all about character and story.

I don't live full-time in Scotland. I'm mostly in the US and I sometimes think of living in California, or Mexico, or Berlin. If I go somewhere and I like it, I often wonder what it would be like to live there. But there are always some things I miss about being in Scotland – things like haggis and black pudding and a really good fish supper. The Scottish diet can be pretty good and it's getting better. People still eat a lot of crap but they do that everywhere.

I have a flat in Edinburgh and I go back for two or three months every year so I haven't left Scotland, and with Skype and Twitter and the internet I'm constantly in touch. My two oldest friends, Dougie and Colin, have been mates since we were six and they are still good pals. Most of my other long-standing pals I have known since schooldays. They have been there for all the changes in life, from when you were daft wee boys to adolescents trying to get off with girls, to going to nightclubs, your first marriage, divorce, your second marriage – they become like family. They've always been supportive of me, and not just them but the community in general. I've never felt that 'tall poppy syndrome' thing against me at all – or if it's there I've been blind to it.

Thinking of my homeland, there is one song I really love called *Raining in Glasgow* written by Dean Owens, a friend from Leith. When I was living in the south of England, it always brought back memories of Scotland in the 1980s and 1990s when I used to go through to Glasgow a lot, going to clubs then back to a mate's flat – often in the rain. There was something mystical about it.

Edinburgh is very special to me. I love the view of the castle when you get out of the station and look up at it. The best view is from Princes Street or Alfred Steet. When you get up close to the castle it's a bit scabby. It's best admired from a distance.

I also love the Wallace Monument in Stirling. I think it's beautiful. You look out at the Trossachs and the river Forth in its infancy, and you see what it's eventually going to be when you get to Leith.

Irvinewelsh.net

@IrvineWelsh

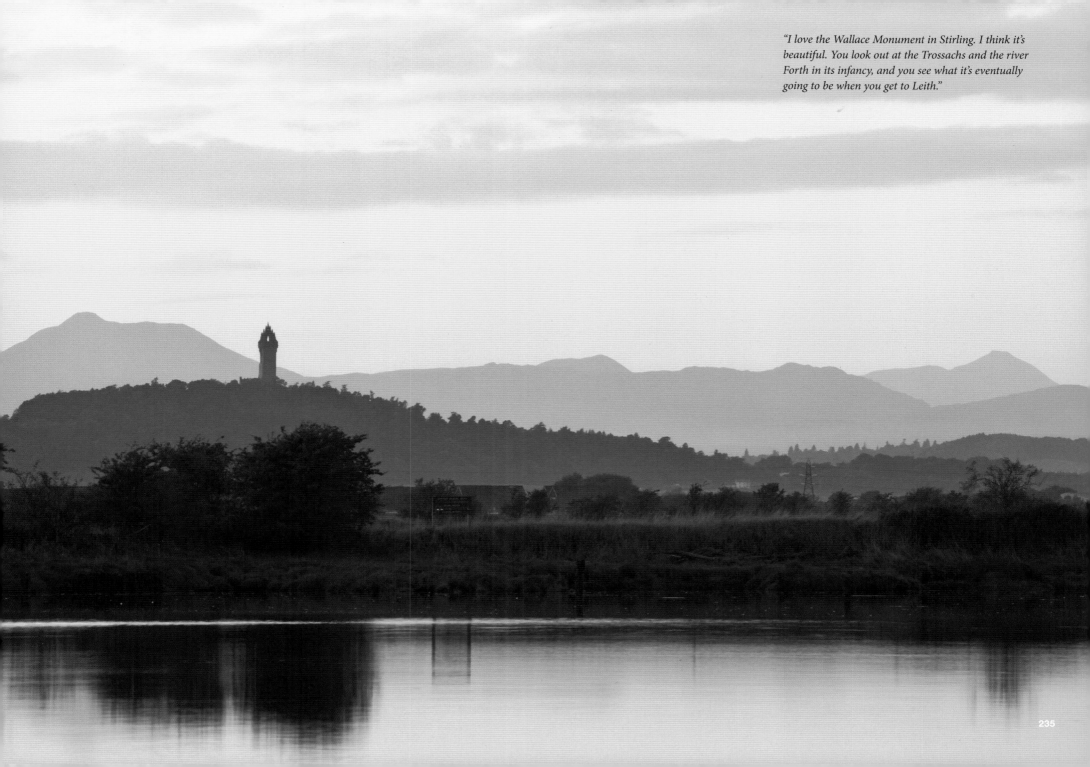

"I love the Wallace Monument in Stirling. I think it's beautiful. You look out at the Trossachs and the river Forth in its infancy, and you see what it's eventually going to be when you get to Leith."

235

ACKNOWLEDGMENTS

This book has been two years in the making, and we are indebted to many people and their organisations who have helped us along the way.

Not least of these are the photographers and photography libraries who supplied the images used throughout this book. Without exception they charged a substantially reduced rate or, in many cases, made no charge at all. Their generosity will help to maximise the potential profits from the book, 90 per cent of which we have pledged to Scottish charities.

Special thanks are due to Visit Scotland and the Daily Record newspaper.

Many individuals have been very helpful and are too numerous to list, but we would like to thank particularly Paul Nicholas, Andy Hall, Shona Hendry from The BIG Partnership, Tommy Gilmour and Vanessa Green.

And, of course, immense thanks to the sons and daughters of Scotland who have given their time to share their memories and favourite places. Without them there would be no book.

PHOTOGRAPHY

David Robertson
scot-image.co.uk

Cover shot and landscape photography on pages: 14, 16, 17, 19, 24, 25, 26, 27, 29, 33, 35, 37, 41, 43, 48, 49, 53, 55, 56, 57, 58, 59, 60, 63, 64, 75, 76, 77, 79, 85, 89, 90, 93, 95, 97, 99, 101, 103, 107, 109, 111, 112, 119, 128, 131, 139, 148, 149, 151, 155, 156, 157, 158, 161, 167, 168, 176, 177, 179, 183, 187, 189, 191, 195, 196, 197, 203, 205, 207, 213, 217, 219, 221, 223, 229, 233, 235

Visit Scotland
visitscotland.com

Landscape photography on pages: 4, 5, 11, 31, 67, 68, 69, 87, 113, 114, 115, 118, 121, 122, 123, 129, 153, 163, 165, 169, 171, 184, 193, 211, 214, 231

Daily Record
dailyrecord.co.uk

Landscape photography on pages: 6, 45, 61, 72, 145, 206

People photographs on pages: 4, 10, 20 (smaller shot), 22, 28, 42, 44, 48, 50, 66, 84 (larger shot), 86, 92, 94, 100 (larger shot), 118, 144, 146, 152, 154, 156, 158, 160 (smaller shot), 162, 168, 170, 184, 186, 190, 204, 212 (larger shot), 214, 216 (smaller shot), 222, 224, 228, 234

Rex Features
rexfeatures.com

Photographs from films or television shows on pages: 116, 120, 160, 208, 210, 220

Andy Hall
andyhallphotography.com

Pages: 28, 51, 81, 117, 159, 181, 188

Sir Malcolm MacGregor
malcolmmacgregor.com

Pages: 124, 125, 126, 127, 142

Gary Brindle
scotaviaimages.co.uk

Pages: 65, 96, 175, 215

Derek Wells
sunshinephotography.co.uk

Pages: 105, 173, 209

Other landscape photograph credits on pages:
7 – Luigi di Pasquale, courtesy of Glasgow Theatre Royal; 9 – Mark Jackson, courtesy of East Lothian Council; 13 – Cameron McVean @camthebam66; 15 – courtesy of Carnegie Hall; 21 – George Donohoe; 23 – Thomas Haywood, courtesy of Marketing Edinburgh; 39 – Gordon Buchanan; 47 – Crown copyright reproduced courtesy of Historic Scotland; 52, 54 – Sylvia Taylor; 71 – Reza Najafi; 73 – courtesy of Glasgow City Council; 82, 83 – Rangers Football Club; 91 – Waverley Excursions; 133 – MacLeod Estate; 135 – Callanish Digital Designs; 136, 137 – Dr Sue Hamstead, Wemyss Caves; 141 – karenbrodiephotography.co.uk;

143 – Duart Castle, Isle of Mull; 147 – christopherswan.co.uk; 185 – courtesy of Marketing Edinburgh; 198, 199 – Marianne Mitchelson; 201 – Nisbet Wylie; 202 – Hanneke Scott Van Wel; 225 – Richard Newton Photography; 227 – Cameron McVean @camthebam66

Except where listed above, most photographs of the celebrities have been provided by themselves or their representatives.

Credits for other photographs of celebrities on pages: 20 (larger shot) – George Donohoe; 36, 38 – Gordon Buchanan; 60 – Donovan Discs 2015; 62 – Michael Collopy, Donovan Discs 2015 (portrait), Album Art copyright 2015, Donovan Discs 2015 (album cover); 72, 74 – Corey Nickols; 76 – Bob McDevitt Photography; 78 – Dan Towers of Onedition Media, UK Sport; 80 – Rangers Football Club; 92 (cat) – Eaglestirreth (see Flickr); 96, 98 – paulcoxphotos.co.uk; 108, 110 – Manchester United Football Club; 128 – Carol Ann Peacock; 130 – Peter Sandground; 132, 134 – copyright MacLeod Estate; 150 – Pete Dunwell; 172 – Brian Aris; 174 – Carol Ann Peacock; 176, 178 – DC Thomson & Co Ltd; 182 – courtesy of Edinburgh Lyceum Theatre; 196 – Marianne Mitchelson; 218 – Qdos Entertainment

INDEX OF PLACES

Aberdeen 77, 109, 167

Abernethy Forest 39

Angus, standing stones 198, 199

Antonine Way, Croy 47

Arran 5, 107

Aviemore 184

Ayr. .61, 65

Blair Atholl 157

Broughty Castle 168

Carter Bar 11

Cramond 13

Crieff. 118

Cromarty Firth 171

Culzean Castle 176

Dundee . . . . 49 (view towards), 231

Dunfermline . . . . .15 (Carnegie Hall),
. . . . 57 (Abbey Church)

Dunure Castle 67

Durness 16, 17

East Wemyss caves 136, 137

Edinburgh 14, 19, 23, 24, 48, 55, 58,
. . . . 71, 76, 81, 185, 187, 229, 233

Eildon Hills. 27

Eilean Donan Castle 41

Eriska, Isle of 163

Eshaness 113

Falkland Palace, Fife. 56

Falkirk, The Kelpies 201

Fife, aerial view 227

Fort William 177

Forth bridges 175

Foula 52

Glasgow 6, 7, 45, 58, 63, 72, 73, 75, 79, 82,
. . . . 83, 85, 87, 95, 96, 105, 145, 153,
. . . . 173, 188, 191, 203, 209, 217, 219

Glencoe 33, 142, 183

Glennifer Braes 141

Grangemouth 64

Great Cumbrae Island 181

Haylie Brae 147

Heavy Horse, M8 motorway 202

Inchmahome Priory 165

Islay 43, 60, 189

John Muir Country Park 68

John O' Groats 214, 215

Kippford 211

Kinnoull Hill, Perth 51

Lady Mary's Walk 117

Lamlash 28, 29

Largo Law 193

Largs 169

Leven beach. 225

Leverburgh 129

Lewis 112, 128

Loch Earn 119

Loch Fyne 123

Loch Katrine. 99

Loch Lomond 155, 213

Loch Ness. 179

Lossiemouth. 159

Luskentyre, Harris 131

Luss. 103

Melrose Abbey 59

Millport 122

Mull . . . . 37 (Tobermory),
. . . . 143 (Duart Castle), 223 (Kintra)

Mull of Kintyre 207

Musselburgh. 9

Outer Hebrides 127, 135

Pass of the Cattle 114, 115

Plockton 221

Rest and be Thankful 206

River Findhorn 124

Rothesay (on Waverley) 91

St Abbs 69

St Andrews 101, 195

St Ninian's Isle 53

Saltcoats 121

Scalloway 54

Seil Island 89

Smailholm Tower 26

Skye 93, 133, 134, 148, 149, 151

Spean Bridge 25

Stirling Castle 196

Stonehaven 111

Suilven Mountain 139

Torridon 125

Troon 4

Trossachs 97, 205

Turnberry golf course 31

Ullapool 17

Wallace Monument 161, 197, 235

Wester Ross 35

West Highland Way 90

West Kilbride 20, 21